Religion's Sudden Decline

T0355170

The red line on this book's front cover shows the rise and decline of the Aggregate Religiosity Index in the US, from 1937 to 2019. Developed by J. Tobin Grant, this index is based on seventeen indicators of religiosity and is estimated for each year despite missing values. For more details, see Figure 7.10 in Chapter 7.

Religion's Sudden Decline

What's Causing it, and What Comes Next?

RONALD F. INGLEHART

OXFORD
UNIVERSITY PRESS

OXFORD
UNIVERSITY PRESS

Oxford University Press is a department of the University of Oxford. It furthers
the University's objective of excellence in research, scholarship, and education
by publishing worldwide. Oxford is a registered trade mark of Oxford University
Press in the UK and certain other countries.

Published in the United States of America by Oxford University Press
198 Madison Avenue, New York, NY 10016, United States of America.

Library of Congress Cataloging-in-Publication Data
Names: Inglehart, Ronald, author.
Title: Religion's sudden decline : what's causing it,
and what comes next? / Ronald F. Inglehart.
Description: New York, NY : Oxford University Press, 2021. |
Includes bibliographical references and index.
Identifiers: LCCN 2020027037 (print) | LCCN 2020027038 (ebook) |
ISBN 9780197547045 (hardback) | ISBN 9780197547052 (paperback) |
ISBN 9780197547076 (epub) | ISBN 9780197547083
Subjects: LCSH: Religion—History—21st century. | Religion—Forecasting. |
Scandinavia—Religion. | Religion and sociology—Scandinavia. |
Secularism—Political aspects—Scandinavia. |
Political culture—Scandinavia.
Classification: LCC BL51 .I624 2021 (print) | LCC BL51 (ebook) |
DDC 200.9/05—dc23
LC record available at https://lccn.loc.gov/2020027037
LC ebook record available at https://lccn.loc.gov/2020027038

DOI: 10.1093/oso/9780197547045.001.0001

3 5 7 9 8 6 4 2

Paperback printed by Sheridan Books, Inc., United States of America
Hardback printed by Bridgeport National Bindery, Inc., United States of America

*This book is dedicated with love to my wife, Marita,
and to my children Milo, Ronald, Rachel, Elizabeth and Sylvia*

Contents

Contents

Preface

The economic and cultural changes linked with modernization tend to bring declining emphasis on religion—and in high-income societies this process recently reached a tipping point at which it accelerates. This book tests these claims against empirical evidence from countries containing 90 percent of the world's population, explaining why this is happening and exploring what will come next.

Secularization has accelerated. From 1981 to 2007, most countries became more religious—but from 2007 to 2020, the overwhelming majority became *less* religious. For centuries, all major religions encouraged norms that limit women to producing as many children as possible and discourage any sexual behavior not linked with reproduction. These norms were needed when facing high infant mortality and low life expectancy but require suppressing strong drives and are rapidly eroding. These norms are so strongly linked with religion that abandoning them undermines religiosity. Religion became pervasive because it was conducive to survival, encouraged sharing when there was no social security system, and is conducive to mental health and coping with insecure conditions. People need coherent belief systems, but religion is declining.

The Nordic countries have consistently been at the cutting edge of cultural change and can provide an idea of what lies ahead. They were initially shaped by Protestantism, but their 20th-century social democratic welfare systems added universal health coverage; high levels of state support for education, welfare spending, child care, and pensions; and an ethos of social solidarity. The Nordic countries are also characterized by rapidly declining religiosity. Does this portend corruption and nihilism? Apparently not. These countries lead the world on numerous indicators of a well-functioning society, including economic equality, gender equality, low homicide rates, subjective well-being, environmental protection, and democracy. They have become less religious, but their people have high levels of interpersonal trust, tolerance, honesty, social solidarity, and commitment to democratic norms. The decline of religiosity has far-reaching implications. This book explores what comes next.

These findings build on previous work with Pippa Norris, particularly *Sacred and Secular: Religion and Politics Worldwide* (Norris & Inglehart, 2004/2011). Despite *Sacred and Secular*'s relatively recent publication, major changes have occurred since it appeared, and these changes shed new light on how religion is evolving.

I express my gratitude to the people who made the present book possible by carrying out the World Values Survey (WVS) and the European Values Study (EVS) in over 100 countries, from 1981 to 2020. My heartfelt thanks go to the following WVS and EVS principal investigators for creating and sharing this rich and complex dataset: Salvatore Abbruzzese, Abdel-Hamid Abdel-Latif, Anthony M. Abela, Marchella Abrasheva, Javier J. Hernández Acosta, Olda Acuna, Mohammen Addahri, Q. K. Ahmad, Pervaiz Ahmed, Alisher Aldashev, Darwish Abdulrahman Al-Emadi, Abdulrazaq Ali, Fathi Ali, Rasa Alishauskene, Harry Anastasiou, Helmut Anheier, Jose Arocena, Wil A. Art, Soo Young Auh, Taghi Azadarmaki, Ljiljana Bacevic, Richard Bachia-Caruana, Erik Baekkeskov, Yuri Bakaloff, Olga Balakireva, Josip Baloban, David Barker, Miguel Basanez, Elena Bashkirova, Abdallah Bedaida, Jorge Benitez, Miloš Bešić, Jaak Billiet, Alan Black, Eduard Bomhoff, Ammar Boukhedir, Rahma Bourquia, Fares al Braizat, Lori Bramwell-Jones, Michael Breen, Ziva Broder, Thawilwadee Bureekul, Karin Bush, Harold Caballeros, Maria Silvestre Cabrera, Claudio Calvaruso, Pavel Campeaunu, Augustin Canzani, Daniel Capistrano, Giuseppe Capraro, Marita Carballo, Andres Casas, Nora Castillo, Henrique Carlos de O. de Castro, Chih-Jou Jay Chen, Pi-Chao Chen, Edmund W. Cheng, Pradeep Chhibber, Mark F. Chingono, Hei-yuan Chiu, Vincent Chua, Constanza Cilley, Margit Cleveland, Mircea Comsa, Munqith Dagher, Núria Segués Daina, Andrew P. Davidson, Herman De Dijn, Pierre Delooz, Nikolas Demertzis, Ruud de Moor, Carlos Denton, Xavier Depouilly, Peter J. D. Derenth, Abdel Nasser Djabi, Karel Dobbelaere, Hermann Duelmer, Anna Mia Ekstroem, Javier Elzo, Maria Fernanda Endara, Yilmaz Esmer, Paul Estgen, Marim Fagbemi, Tony Fahey, Nadjematul Faizah, Tair Faradov, Roberto Stefan Foa, Michael Fogarty, Georgy Fotev, Juis de Franca, Morten Frederiksen, Aikaterini Gari, Ilir Gedeshi, James Georgas, C. Geppaart, Bilai Gilani, Mark Gill, Timothy Gravelle, Stjepan Gredlj, Renzo Gubert, Linda Luz Guerrero, Peter Gundelach, David Sulmont Haak, Rabih Haber, Christian Haerpfer, Abdelwahab Ben Hafaiedh, Jacques Hagenaars, Loek Halman, Mustafa Hamarneh, Tracy Hammond, Sang-Jin Han, Elemer Hankiss, Olafur Haraldsson, Stephen Harding, Mari Harris, Mazen Hassan, Pierre Hausman, Bernadette C. Hayes, Gordon Heald, Ricardo

Manuel Hermelo, Camilo Herrera, Felix Heunks, Virginia Hodgkinson, Hanh Hoang Hong, Nadra Muhammed Hosen, Joan Rafel Mico Ibanez, Kenji Iijima, Kenichi Ikeda, Fr. Joe Inganuez, Ljubov Ishimova, Wolfgang Jagodzinski, Meril James, Aleksandra Jasinska-Kania, Will Jennings, Anders Jenssen, Guðbjörg Jónsdóttir, Fridrik Jonsson, Dominique Joye, Stanislovas Juknevicius, Salue Kalikova, Tatiana Karabchuk, Kieran Kennedy, Jan Kerkhofs S.J., Kimmo Ketola, Nail Khaibulin, J. F. Kielty, Hans-Dieter Kilngemann, Johann Kinghorn, Kseniya Kizilova, Renate Kocher, Joanna Konieczna, Sokratis Koniordos, Hennie Kotze, Hanspeter Kriesi, Sylvia Kritzinger, Miori Kurimura, Zuzana Kusá, Marta Lagos, Bernard Lategan, Francis Lee, Grace Lee, Michel Legrand, Carlos Lemoine, Noah Lewin-Epstein, Vladymir Joseph Licudine, Ruud Lijkx, Juan Linz, Ola Listhaug, Jin-yun Liu, Leila Lotti, Susanne Lundasen, Toni Makkai, Brina Malnar, Heghine Manasyan, Robert Manchin, Mahar Mangahas, Mario Marinov, Mirosława Marody, Carlos Matheus, Robert Mattes, Ian McAllister, Nathalie Mendez, Rafael Mendizabal, Tianguang Meng, Jon Miller, Felipe Miranda, Mansoor Moaddel, Mustapha Mohammed, Jose Molina, Daniel E. Moreno Morales, Alejandro Moreno, Gaspar K. Munishi, Naasson Munyandamutsa, Kostas Mylonas, Neil Nevitte, Chun Hung Ng, Simplice Ngampou, Jaime Medrano Nicolas, Juan Diez Nicolas, Dionysis Nikolaou, Elisabeth Noelle-Neumann, Pippa Norris, Elone Nwabuzor, Stephen Olafsson, Muzzafar Olimov, Saodat Olimova, Francisco Andres Orizo, Magued Osman, Merab Pachulia, Christina Paez, Alua Pankhurst, Dragomir Pantic, Juhani Pehkonen, Paul Perry, E. Petersen, Antoanela Petkovska, Doru Petruti, Thorleif Pettersson, Pham Minh Hac, Pham Thanh Nghi, Timothy Phillips, Gevork Pogosian, Eduard Ponarin, Lucien Pop, Bi Puranen, Ladislav Rabusic, Andrei Raichev, Botagoz Rakisheva, Alice Ramos, Sonia Ranincheski, Anu Realo, Tim Reeskens, Jan Rehak, Helene Riffault, Ole Riis, Ferruccio Biolcati Rinaldi, Angel Rivera-Ortiz, Nils Rohme, Catalina Romero, Gergely Rosta, David Rotman, Victor Roudometof, Giancarlo Rovati, Samir Abu Ruman, Andrus Saar, Erki Saar, Aida Saidani, Pepita Batalla Salvadó, Ratchawadee Sangmahamad, Rajab Sattarov, Vivian Schwarz, Paolo Segatti, Rahmat Seigh, Tan Ern Ser, Sandeep Shastri, Shen Mingming, Jill Sheppard, Musa Shteivi, Renata Siemienska, Richard Sinnott, Alan Smith, Natalia Soboleva, Ahmet Sozen, Michèle Ernst Stähli, Gerry Stocker, Jean Stoetzel, Kancho Stoichev, Marin Stoychev, Katarina Strapcová, John Sudarsky, Edward Sullivan, Ni Wayan Suriastini, Marc Swyngedouw, Tang Ching-Ping, Farooq Tanwir, Jean-Francois Tchernia, Kareem Tejumola, Jorge Villamor Tigno, Noel

Timms, Larissa Titarenko, Miklos Tomka, Alfredo Torres, Niko Tos, Istvan Gyorgy Toth, Jorge Aragón Trelles, Joseph Troisi, Ming-Chang Tsai, Tu Su-hao, Claudiu Tufis, Samo Uhan, Jorge Vala, Andrei Vardomatskii, Nino Veskovic, Amaru Villanueva, Manuel Villaverde, David Voas, Bogdan Voicu, Malina Voicu, Liliane Voye, Richard M. Walker, Alan Webster, Friedrich Welsch, Christian Welzel, Meidam Wester, Chris Whelan, Christof Wolf, Stan Wong, Robert Worcester, Seiko Yamazaki, Dali Yang, Jie Yang, Birol Yesilada, Ephraim Yuchtman-Yaar, Josefina Zaiter, Catalin Zamfir, Margarita Zavadskaya, Brigita Zepa, Nursultan Zhamgyrchiev, Yang Zhong, Ruta Ziliukaite, Ignacio Zuasnabar, and Paul Zulehner.

The WVS and EVS data used in this book consists of 423 surveys carried out in successive waves from 1981 to 2020 in 112 countries and territories containing over 90 percent of the world's population.[1] Building on the EuroBarometer surveys founded by Jacques-Rene Rabier, Jan Kerkhofs and Ruud de Moor organized the EVS and invited me to organize similar surveys in other parts of the world, which led to the founding of the WVS. Jaime Diez Medrano has done a superb job in archiving both the WVS and the EVS datasets and making them available to hundreds of thousands of users, who have analyzed and downloaded the data from the WVS and EVS websites.

I am grateful to Jon Miller, Arthur Lupia, Kenneth Kollman, and other colleagues at the University of Michigan for comments and suggestions. I also am grateful to Anna Cotter, Yujeong Yang, and Anil Menon for superb research assistance, and I gratefully acknowledge support from the U.S. National Science Foundation, the Bill and Melinda Gates Foundation, and the foreign ministries of Sweden and the Netherlands, each of which supported fieldwork for the WVS in a number of countries where funding from local sources was unavailable. I also thank the Russian Ministry of Education and Science for a grant that made it possible to found the Laboratory for Comparative Social Research at the Higher School of Economics in Moscow and St. Petersburg, and to carry out the WVS in Russia and several Soviet successor countries. Finally, I am grateful to the University of Michigan's Amy and Alan Loewenstein Professorship in Democracy and Human Rights, which supported research assistance for this work.

1

The Shift from Pro-Fertility Norms
to Individual-Choice Norms

Secularization has recently accelerated in most countries, for reasons inherent in the current phase of modernization. This book tests this claim
against empirical evidence from surveys carried out from 1981 to 2020, in
over 100 countries containing more than 90 percent of the world's population
and covering all major cultural zones. This chapter gives an overview of the
book's findings. The empirical evidence is presented in subsequent chapters.

Secularization recently accelerated. Not long ago, Norris and Inglehart
(2004/2011) analyzed religious change in 49 countries from which a substantial time series of survey evidence was available from 1981 to 2007. (These
countries contain 60 percent of the world's population.)[1] They found that the
publics of 33 out of 49 countries had become more religious during this period. When these same 49 countries were reexamined in 2020, the trend toward rising religiosity had reversed itself. As Figure 1.1 indicates, in 2020 the
publics of only six countries showed net gains in religiosity since 2007; one
showed no significant change; and the publics of 42 countries had become
less religious from 2007 to 2020.

For many years, the U.S. has been cited as the key piece of evidence demonstrating that even highly modernized countries can be strongly religious.
But since 2007, the U.S. has been secularizing more rapidly than any other
country for which we have data. Its level has fallen substantially by virtually
every measure of religiosity, and by one widely recognized criterion it now
ranks as the 12th *least* religious country in the world.

There are several reasons secularization is accelerating. One generally
overlooked cause springs from the fact that, for many centuries, a coherent
set of pro-fertility norms* evolved in most countries that assigns women
the role of producing as many children as possible and discourages divorce,

---

* Governments sometimes adopt pro-natalist policies intended to raise the country's birth rate.
Pro-fertility norms are cultural traditions with strong moral connotations, often backed by religion.

Religion's Sudden Decline. Ronald F. Inglehart, Oxford University Press (2021). © Oxford University Press.
DOI: 10.1093/oso/9780197547045.003.0001

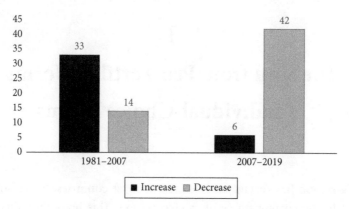

Figure 1.1 Countries showing increasing and decreasing religiosity over two
time periods.
Source: Responses to question "How important is God in your life?" asked in the World Values
Survey and European Values Study. See Figures 7.3, 7.4, and 7.5 for fuller details.

abortion, homosexuality, contraception, and any other form of sexual behavior not linked with reproduction.

Virtually all major world religions instill pro-fertility norms, which helped
societies survive when facing high infant mortality and low life expectancy.
These norms require people to suppress strong natural urges but are no longer
needed for societal survival—and are rapidly giving way to individual-choice
norms, supporting gender equality and tolerance of divorce, abortion, and
homosexuality. Pro-fertility norms are so closely linked with traditional religious worldviews that abandoning them undermines religiosity. This rapid
change of basic societal norms creates a polarization between those with traditional worldviews and those with modern worldviews, producing bitter
political conflict.

Rising support for individual-choice norms is not the only factor driving
secularization. Reactions against religious fundamentalists' embrace of xenophobic authoritarian politicians, against the Roman Catholic Church's
long history of covering up child abuse, and against terrorism by religious
extremists, all seem to be contributing to secularization. In the U.S., for
example, since the 1990s the Republican Party has sought to win support
by adopting the Christian conservative position on sexual morality and
opposition to same-sex marriage and abortion and closed ranks behind
President Donald Trump's authoritarian xenophobic policies. Some critics
argued that this didn't just attract religious voters—it was also driving

social liberals, especially young ones, away from religion (Hout & Fischer, 2002). Initially, this claim seemed dubious because there is a large and well-founded literature on how religion shapes politics. A person's religion was generally so stable that it was almost a genetic attribute. But as religion weakens, the dominant causal flow can change direction, with one's political views increasingly shaping one's religious outlook. Thus, using General Social Survey panel data, Hout and Fischer (2014) found that people were not becoming more secular and then moving toward liberal politics to fit their new religious identity; instead, they found that the main causal direction runs from politics to religion. Younger respondents were disproportionately likely to desert the Republican Party because of a growing desire for personal autonomy, particularly concerning sex, abortion, and drugs. As another observer recently put it, "Politics can drive whether you identify with a faith, how strongly you identify with that faith, and how religious you are . . . and some people on the left are falling away from religion because they see it as so wrapped up with Republican politics" (Margolis, 2018). A number of factors (including some nation-specific ones) help explain the recent worldwide decline of religion—but the rise of individual-choice norms seems to be the most widely applicable one.

This book focuses on one important aspect of social change: the changing role of religion. Another book, *Cultural Evolution: People's Motivations Are Changing, and Changing the World* (R. F. Inglehart, 2018), provides a broader framework for understanding how economic and technological development are reshaping the world, analyzing changes in basic values concerning politics, economic inequality, gender roles, child-rearing norms, religion, willingness to fight for one's country, and the implications for society of the rise of artificial intelligence. It interprets these developments from the perspective of evolutionary modernization theory.

Well into the 20th century, leading social thinkers held that religious beliefs would decline as scientific knowledge and rationality spread throughout the world. The worldviews of most scientists were indeed transformed by the spread of scientific knowledge, but religion persisted among the general public. In recent years, the dramatic activism of fundamentalist movements in many countries and the religious revival in former communist countries have made it obvious that religion is not disappearing, and even led to claims of a global resurgence of religion.

An influential challenge to the secularization thesis, religious markets theory, argues that established churches become complacent monopolies—but competition between churches brings high levels of religious participation (Finke & Iannaccone, 1993; Stark & Bainbridge, 1985). Still another perspective, the religious individualization thesis, claims that the declining influence of churches does not represent a declining role for religion; people are simply freeing themselves from institutional guidelines and making their own choices, with subjective forms of religion replacing institutionalized ones.

Norris and Inglehart (2004/2011) propose an alternative to all three versions of secularization theory, arguing that insecure people need the psychological support and reassuring predictability of traditional religion's absolute rules—but that as survival becomes more secure, this need is reduced. They present evidence that industrialization, urbanization, growing prosperity, and other aspects of modernization are conducive to secularization. Nevertheless, they point out, the world as a whole now has more people with traditional religious views than it did 50 years ago because, while virtually all major religions encourage high birth rates, secularization has a strong negative impact on them. Today, virtually all high-income societies are relatively secular, and their birth rates have fallen below the population-replacement level—but low-income societies remain religious and are producing large numbers of children. Modernization brings secularization, but contrasting birth rates maintain the number of believers—at least for the time being, since birth rates are falling even in low-income countries.

Despite differential fertility rates, secularization has persisted, and has recently accelerated in much of the world, largely because of two related cultural shifts:

1. Insecure people need the predictability and absolute rules of traditional religion—and throughout history, survival has usually been insecure. But modernization brings greater prosperity, lower rates of violence, and improved public health, reducing the demand for religion. The second factor has accelerated this trend.
2. A shift from pro-fertility norms to individual-choice norms. The world's major religions inculcated pro-fertility norms in order to replace the population when facing high infant mortality and low life expectancy. These norms require strong self-denial, but rising life expectancy and sharply declining infant mortality have made these norms no longer necessary for societal survival. After an intergenerational time lag, pro-fertility norms, emphasizing traditional gender roles and stigmatizing

any sexual behavior not linked with reproduction, are giving way to individual-choice norms supporting gender equality and tolerance of divorce, abortion, and homosexuality. This is eroding traditional religious worldviews.

Instead of attributing secularization to the advance of scientific knowledge or to modernization in general— both of which imply that secularization is a universal and unidirectional process—evolutionary modernization theory argues that secularization reflects rising levels of security. It occurs in countries that have attained high levels of existential security and can move in reverse if societies experience prolonged periods of declining security.

Moreover, evolutionary modernization theory recognizes that modernization is path-dependent, with a given country's level of religiosity reflecting its historical heritage. For example, though most countries' historically dominant belief system was religious, Confucian-influenced societies were shaped by a secular belief system that made their starting level of religiosity lower than that of other countries—where it remains today.

Security is psychological as well as physical. The collapse of a belief system can reduce people's sense of security as much as war or economic hardship does. Religion traditionally compensated for low levels of economic and physical security by providing assurance that the world was in the hands of an infallible higher power who ensured that, if one followed his rules, things would ultimately work out for the best. Marxist ideology replaced religion for many people, assuring its believers that history was on their side and that their cause would ultimately triumph. The collapse of Marxist belief systems led to a massive decline of subjective well-being among the people of the former Soviet Empire, a decline that lasted for decades, leaving an ideological vacuum to be filled by rising religiosity and nationalism.

Finally, though secularization normally occurs at the pace of intergenerational population replacement, it can reach a tipping point where the dominant opinion shifts, and the forces of conformism and social desirability start to favor the outlook they once opposed—producing rapid cultural change. Younger and better-educated groups in high-income countries have reached this point.

Alexander et al. (2016) argue that the legalization of abortion and same-sex marriage are part of a long-term trend toward giving people a wider range of choice in all aspects of life—but that until recently, religion generally managed to block this trend in one important domain, that of sexual freedom. They suggest that more secure living conditions, from rising life expectancy to broader education, have led to cultural changes that allow a wider range of choices. This trend has begun to spill over into the realm of sexual freedom, where, until recently, religious norms and institutions were able to resist the spread of free choice. They support these claims with a broad array of evidence. Since the Enlightenment, the struggle for human emancipation—from the abolition of slavery to the recognition of human rights—has been a defining feature of modernization (Markoff, 1996; Pinker, 2011). This struggle virtually always aroused resistance from reactionary forces (Armstrong, 2001; Weinberg & Pedahzur, 2004). Nevertheless, social movements and civil society groups around the world have continued to campaign for human emancipation, pushing its frontier farther and farther (Carter, 2012; Clark, 2009). This frontier has reached the domain of individual-choice norms, where religion until recently had largely succeeded in blocking the spread of free choice (Frank et al., 2010; Kafka, 2005; Knudsen, 2006). The recent legalization of abortion and same-sex marriage in many countries constitutes a breakthrough at society's most basic level: its ability to reproduce itself. These changes are driven by growing mass support for sexual self-determination, which is part of an even broader trend toward greater emphasis on freedom of choice in all aspects of life. Support for free choice in the realm of sexual behavior has emerged relatively recently and is now moving rapidly, but it remains hotly contested by conservative social forces, especially religion.

Throughout history, sexual reproduction has been an aspect of life in which religious tradition has most successfully blocked the spread of free choice. The rise of free choice in this domain constitutes an evolutionary breakthrough in the development of moral systems (Alexander et al., 2016). Today, Western countries' social norms are profoundly different from those of the postwar era. In 1945, homosexuality was still criminal in most Western countries; it is now legal in virtually all of them. In the postwar era, both church attendance and birth rates were high; today, church attendance has declined drastically and human fertility rates have fallen below the population-replacement level.

Although deep-seated norms limiting women's roles and stigmatizing homosexuality persisted from biblical times to the 20th century, the World Values Survey and the European Values Study show rapid changes from 1981 to 2020 in high-income countries, with growing acceptance of gender equality and LGBTQ people and a rapid decline of religiosity. In low-income societies, tolerance of abortion, homosexuality, and divorce remains low, and conformist pressures inhibit people from expressing tolerance. And in most former communist countries, religion grew rapidly after 1990, filling the vacuum left by the collapse of Marxist belief systems—and encouraging a return to traditional pro-fertility norms.

But intergenerational population replacement has made individual-choice norms increasingly acceptable—initially among the younger and better-educated strata of high-income societies. Experimentation with new norms occurs, and when it seems successful, spreads—with the prevailing outlook gradually shifting from rejection to acceptance of the new norms. As attitudes become more tolerant, more gays and lesbians come out. Growing numbers of people realize that some of the people they know and like are homosexual, leading them to become more tolerant and encouraging more LGBTQ people to come out, in a positive feedback loop (Andersen & Fetner, 2008; R. Inglehart and Welzel, 2005).

Religiosity and the Shift from Pro-Fertility Norms to Individual-Choice Norms

Religion is not an unchanging aspect of human nature. The belief in a God who is concerned with human moral conduct becomes prevalent only with the emergence of agricultural societies. Concepts of God have continued to evolve since biblical times, from an angry tribal God who was placated by human sacrifice and demanded genocide, to a benevolent God whose laws applied to all humanity. Thousands of societies have existed, most of which are now extinct. Virtually all of them had high infant mortality rates and low life expectancy, making it necessary to produce large numbers of children in order to replace the population. And virtually all societies that survived for long inculcated pro-fertility norms limiting women to the roles of wife and mother and stigmatizing divorce, abortion, homosexuality, masturbation, and any other sexual behavior not linked with reproduction (Nolan & Lenski, 2015). From biblical times to the 20th century, some societies have advocated celibacy, but these societies have disappeared. Virtually all major religions that survive today instill gender roles and reproductive norms that encourage women to cede leadership roles to men and to bear and raise as many children as possible—stigmatizing any sexual behavior not linked with reproduction.

Throughout history, religion has helped people cope with survival under insecure conditions. Facing starvation, violence, or disease, it assured people that the future was in the hands of an infallible god and that if they followed his rules, things would work out. This gave people the courage to cope with threatening and unpredictable situations rather than give way to despair, increasing their chances of survival. Having a clear belief system is conducive to physical and mental health, and religious people tend to be happier than nonreligious people (R. F. Inglehart, 2018, Chapter 8). The belief system need not be religious; Marxism once provided a clear belief system and hope for the future for many people—but when it collapsed, subjective well-being collapsed along with it.

Since World War II, survival has become increasingly secure for a growing share of the world's population. Income and life expectancy have been rising and poverty and illiteracy have been declining throughout the world since 1970, and crime rates have been declining for many decades. The world is now experiencing the longest period without war between major powers in recorded history. This, together with the postwar economic miracles and the emergence of the welfare state, produced conditions under which a large share of those born since 1945 in Western Europe, North America, Japan, Australia, and New Zealand grew up taking survival for granted, bringing intergenerational shifts toward new, more permissive values.

Most societies no longer require high fertility rates. Infant mortality has fallen to a tiny fraction of its 1950 level. Effective birth control technology, labor-saving devices, improved child care facilities, and low infant mortality make it possible for women to have children and full-time careers. Traditional pro-fertility norms are giving way to individual-choice norms that allow people a broader range of choice in how to live their lives.

Pro-fertility norms have high costs. Forcing women to stay in the home and gays and lesbians to stay in the closet requires severe repression. Once high human fertility rates are no longer needed, there are strong incentives to move away from pro-fertility norms—which usually means moving away from religion. As this book demonstrates, norms concerning gender equality, divorce, abortion, and homosexuality are changing rapidly. Young people in high-income societies are increasingly aware of the tension between religion and individual-choice norms, motivating them to reject religion. Beginning in 2010, secularization has accelerated sharply.

A long time lag intervened between the point when high fertility rates were no longer needed to replace the population and the point when these changes occurred. People hesitate to give up familiar norms governing gender roles and sexual behavior. But when a society reaches a sufficiently high level of economic and physical security that younger birth cohorts grow up taking survival for granted, it opens the way for an intergenerational shift from pro-fertility norms to individual-choice norms that encourages secularization. Although basic values normally change at the pace of intergenerational population replacement, the shift from pro-fertility norms to individual-choice norms has reached a tipping point at which conformist pressures reverse polarity and are accelerating changes they once resisted.

Different aspects of cultural change are moving at different rates. In recent years, high-income countries have been experiencing massive immigration by previously unfamiliar groups. They have also been experiencing rising inequality and declining job security, for reasons linked with the winner-takes-all economies of advanced knowledge societies. The causes of rising inequality are abstract and poorly understood, but immigrants can be clearly visible, making it easy for demagogues to blame them for the disappearance of secure, well-paid jobs. In fact, immigrants are disproportionately likely to create new jobs; for instance, about half of the entrepreneurs in Silicon Valley are foreign-born. But psychological reactions do not necessarily reflect rational analysis. Moreover, many recent immigrants are Muslim, and hostility to them is compounded by highly publicized Islamic terrorism. Accordingly, though acceptance of gays and lesbians and gender equality has risen in most developed countries, xenophobia remains widespread. Coupled with a reaction against rapid cultural change, this has enabled anti-immigrant parties to win a large share of the vote in many countries.

Religion became pervasive because it was conducive to societal survival in many different ways. It minimized internal conflict by establishing rules against theft, deceit, and murder and other forms of violence, encouraged norms of sharing, and instilled pro-fertility norms that encouraged reproduction rates high enough to replace the population. Religions were not the only belief system that could accomplish this. In much of East Asia, a secular Confucian belief system became widespread that did not rely on a moral God who imposed rewards and punishments in an afterlife; the Confucian bureaucracy provided rewards and punishments in this world, but they were linked with a set of duties that supported obedience to the state and included the duty to produce a male heir, which encouraged pro-fertility norms.

But pro-fertility norms usually are closely linked with religion. In societies that survive for long, religion imposes strong sanctions on anyone who violates them. Support for pro-fertility norms and religiosity is strongest in insecure societies, especially those with high infant mortality rates, and weakest in relatively secure societies. Pro-fertility norms require people to suppress strong drives, creating a built-in tension between them and individual-choice norms. Throughout most of history, natural selection helped impose pro-fertility norms, because societies that lacked them tended to die out.

In *Darwin's Cathedral*, David Sloan Wilson (2002; cf. D. S. Wilson, 2005) proposes an evolutionary theory of religion, holding that religions are best understood as "superorganisms" adapted to succeed in evolutionary competition against others. From this perspective, morality and religion are biologically and culturally evolved adaptations that enable human groups to function effectively. When Wilson first proposed this theory, almost no widely respected biologist believed in group selection. Since the 1960s, the selfish gene model had dominated the field, holding that evolution could take place only at the individual level (Dawkins, 1977). For a society to function, its members must perform services for each other. But members who behave for the good of the group often put themselves at a disadvantage compared with more selfish members of that group, so how can prosocial behaviors evolve? The solution that Darwin proposed in *The Descent of Man* (1871) is that groups containing mostly altruists have a decisive advantage over groups containing mostly selfish individuals, even if selfish individuals have an advantage over altruists within each group.

This might have provided a basis for understanding the evolution of social behavior, but during the 1960s evolutionary biologists were convinced that between-group selection is virtually always weaker than within-group selection. Group selection became a pariah concept, and inclusive fitness theory, evolutionary game theory, and selfish gene theory were all developed to explain the evolution of apparently altruistic behavior in individualistic terms, without involving group selection.

But Wilson persisted, marshaling a variety of evidence demonstrating how religions have enabled people to achieve, through collective action, things that they could not have done alone. Today, the concept that natural selection takes place at both individual and group levels is widely accepted. Its triumph has been so complete that the founder of sociobiology himself, E. O. Wilson (no relation to David), abandoned his original focus on gene-centered evolution to adopt the view that natural selection takes place at both the level of groups and the level of genes. The two Wilsons even became co-authors (D. S. Wilson & Wilson, 2007). Recent research does not show that between-group selection always prevails against within-group selection, but it does show that between-group selection is often important.

Until recently, natural selection helped impose pro-fertility norms. But a growing number of societies have attained high existential security, long life expectancy, and low infant mortality, making pro-fertility norms no longer necessary for societal survival and opening the way for a shift to individual-choice norms. Normally there is a substantial time lag between changing societal conditions and cultural change. The norms one grows up with are familiar and seem natural, and abandoning them brings stress and anxiety, so deep-rooted norms usually change slowly, largely through intergenerational population replacement.

Throughout most of history, religious institutions were able to impose pro-fertility norms. But the causal relationship is reciprocal and the dominant direction can be reversed: if pro-fertility norms come to be seen as outmoded and repressive, their rejection also brings rejection of religion. In societies where support for pro-fertility norms is giving way to individual-choice norms, we find declining religiosity. In societies where religion remains strong, little or no change in pro-fertility norms is taking place. But religiosity has been growing in some societies, particularly in formerly communist societies, and there it has been accompanied by growing emphasis on pro-fertility norms and declining acceptance of individual-choice norms.

The declining need for pro-fertility norms opened the way for gradual secularization, with the young being most open to change. Consequently, in high-income countries the younger birth cohorts are much less religious than their older compatriots; among those born between 1894 and 1903, 42 percent said that God was very important in their lives; among those born between 1994 and 2003, only 11 percent said this.[2] These age differences do not reflect some universal aspect of the human life cycle, through which people grow more religious as they age; such age differences are virtually absent in Muslim-majority countries where little cultural change is occurring. But in high-income countries, we find large and enduring differences between the religiosity of older and younger birth cohorts, and the young do not get more religious as they age.

The Recent Acceleration of Secularization
in High-Income Countries

From 1981 to 2020, the publics of most countries showed rising acceptance of individual-choice norms. This trend reflected a society's level of
existential security: among the high-income countries for which time series data is available, 23 of the 24 countries showed rising acceptance of
individual-choice norms. But this trend was not limited to high-income
countries: the publics of 36 other countries, including seven in Latin
America and some relatively secure ex-communist countries, also showed
rising acceptance of these norms. And the publics of several Muslim-
majority countries have moved from extremely low to slightly higher
levels of acceptance. But the publics of some countries became *less* tolerant
of individual-choice norms; most of these were less secure ex-communist
countries, where religiosity was rising to fill the vacuum left by the collapse of Marxist belief systems.

Today, secularization is largely driven by the shift from pro-fertility
norms to individual-choice norms. The two are closely linked. Countries
whose publics emphasize pro-fertility norms tend to be strongly religious, while countries whose publics emphasize individual-choice norms
are much less religious. As one might expect, the publics of high-income
countries rank highest on individual-choice norms, and—though they
once were far more religious than the people of communist countries—
today they are among the world's least religious peoples. At the other end
of the spectrum, the publics of Muslim-majority countries and low-income
countries in Africa and Latin America are the world's most religious people
and adhere most strongly to pro-fertility norms.

In contrast to the past, the publics of virtually all high-income countries
now rank high on support for individual-choice norms and low on religiosity. This reflects the fact that individual-choice norms and religiosity have
a reciprocal causal connection. Throughout most of history, the causal flow
moved mainly from religion to social norms, enforcing strong taboos on any
sexual behavior not linked with reproduction and limiting women to reproductive roles. But in the 21st century, the main causal flow has begun to move
in the opposite direction, with the publics of a growing number of countries
rejecting traditional pro-fertility norms and consequently becoming less
religious.

How Secularization Accelerates

Our theory implies that (a) in societies where religion remains strong, little or no change in pro-fertility norms will take place; (b) in societies where religiosity is growing, we will find growing support for pro-fertility norms; and (c) in societies where support for pro-fertility norms is rapidly giving way to individual-choice norms, we will find declining religiosity.

Data is available from each of these three types of countries: in Muslim-majority countries, religion remains strong; in most former communist countries, religiosity has grown since the collapse of communism; and in virtually all high-income countries, we find declining religiosity.

Although intergenerational population replacement involves long time lags, cultural change can reach a tipping point at which new norms become dominant. Conformism and social desirability effects then reverse polarity: instead of retarding the changes linked with intergenerational population replacement, they accelerate them, bringing unusually rapid cultural change. In the shift from pro-fertility norms to individual-choice norms, this point has been reached in a growing number of countries, starting with the younger and more secure strata of high-income societies.

Almost all high-income societies have now reached the tipping point where the balance shifts from pro-fertility norms being dominant to individual-choice norms becoming dominant. In 1981, majorities of the public of every country for which we have data endorsed pro-fertility norms—generally by wide margins. But a shift toward individual-choice norms was occurring in high-income countries. In 1990, the Swedish public was the first to cross the tipping point where support for individual-choice norms outweighed support for pro-fertility norms; in subsequent years, the Swedes were followed by the publics of virtually all other high-income countries, with the American public crossing this tipping point only recently.

In high-income countries, support for individual-choice norms is stronger among the young than among the old. In the most recent available survey, the oldest cohort (born before 1933) was still below this tipping point, but the youngest cohort (born since 1994) was far above it. By contrast, the publics of all but the most secure ex-communist countries became *more* religious and less supportive of individual-choice norms. And the publics of all 18 Muslim-majority countries for which data is available remained far below the tipping point at every time point since 1981, continuing to be strongly religious and strongly committed to pro-fertility norms. Shifts in religiosity correspond closely to shifts in the balance between pro-fertility norms and individual-choice norms.

When Norris and Inglehart (2004/2011) examined how much change in religiosity had occurred from 1981 to 2007 in 49 countries for which substantial time series data was then available, they did not find a global resurgence of religion, as many writers had claimed—but they did find that more than two-thirds of the countries for which time series data was available showed rising religiosity in response to the question "How important is God in your life?"[3]

Although the overall trend was upward, the publics of most high-income countries showed *declining* emphasis on religion, and this trend was almost entirely due to intergenerational population replacement. Among the countries showing growing religiosity, the six showing the *most* growth were ex-communist countries, and 13 of the 15 ex-communist countries for which substantial time series data was available showed growing emphasis on religion. Norris and Inglehart (2004/2011) attributed this phenomenon to the severe decline of economic, physical, and psychological security that these societies experienced with the collapse of communism, and to the collapse of the communist ideology, which left many people feeling disoriented and psychologically insecure.

This book updates that analysis with data from the most recent available surveys, carried out more than a decade later. The results show that dramatic changes have occurred since 2007 in the same 49 countries analyzed earlier. In sharp contrast with the earlier findings, which showed the dominant trend to be *rising* religiosity, the data since 2007 shows an overwhelming trend toward *declining* religiosity. The public of virtually every high-income country shifted toward lower levels of religiosity, and many other countries also became less religious. The contrast between ex-communist countries and the rest of the world was weakening, but still the eight countries showing the largest shifts toward *increasing* religiosity from 1981 to 2020 were ex-communist countries.

The most dramatic shift of all was found among the American public, which in 2007 showed virtually no change since 1981—but in the most recent survey showed the largest shift of any country for which we have data, *away* from religion. The United States, a highly developed country that nevertheless had high levels of religiosity, had long been the crucial example demonstrating that modernization need not bring secularization. The wide variety of churches in the United States was said to maximize competition among faiths, demonstrating that where there is competition, there will be vigorous religiosity. The U.S. still has diversity, but since 2007 it has been secularizing at a more rapid rate than any other country for which we have data.

Where religiosity, as measured by the importance of God in one's life, shifted in a given direction, other indicators of religiosity also shifted in the same direction. Thus in the earliest U.S. survey in 1982, 52 percent of the American public said that God was very important in their lives; in 2017, only 23 percent made this choice. In 1982, 83 percent of Americans described themselves as "a religious person"; in 2017, only 55 percent did so. Conversely, in 1982, only 16 percent of Americans said that they "never or practically never" attended religious services; in 2017, 35 percent said that.

The decline of confidence in America's religious institutions was particularly steep, perhaps in response to fundamentalist leaders' uncritical endorsement of right-wing politicians: in 1982, 46 percent of Americans said that they had "a great deal" of confidence in their country's religious institutions; in 2017, only 12 percent said this—only about a fourth as many as in 1982.

These findings support Voas and Chaves's (2016) claim that the United States can no longer be cited as the counterexample that disproves the secularization thesis. Focusing on trends rather than levels, they demonstrate that American religiosity has been declining for decades. And as evidence presented in this book indicates, the U.S. no longer even has exceptionally high *levels* of religiosity.

Formerly communist countries continue to be the main locus of growing religiosity. In 2007, ex-communist countries constituted 13 of the 32 countries with growing religiosity, and in 2019 they constituted 12 of the now only 16 countries in which religiosity was still growing (and all eight of the countries where it was growing most strongly). Though only one formerly communist country switched from the increasingly religious category to the decreasingly religious category, most of them showed smaller net gains in 2019 than they had in 2007. The resurgence of religion in ex-communist countries was losing momentum.

The Muslim-majority countries are a special case. The WVS provides time-series data from ten Muslim-majority countries covering a time span of at least ten years (with a median time span of almost 16 years). These countries show the highest absolute levels of religiosity of any major group, and all of them have mean scores near the top of the scale. But they are not becoming more religious. (There is little room for further growth.) Moreover, although we find large differences between the religiosity of younger and older birth cohorts in high-income countries, age differences are very small in Muslim-majority countries.

Though early secularization theory's emphasis on cognitive factors and the religious markets school's emphasis on the role of religious entrepreneurs probably have some impact on religiosity today, the evidence suggests that emotional factors are considerably more important than entrepreneurs or the spread of scientific information.

Summary

In the 21st century, secularization has accelerated in much of the world, largely because of rising existential security and a shift from pro-fertility norms to individual-choice norms. Pro-fertility norms are no longer needed for societal survival, and individual-choice norms are spreading rapidly in much of the world, undermining religiosity. Other factors also seem to be contributing to the trend, but the impact of rising security and changing social norms seems particularly pervasive.

The fact that religion is currently in retreat has far-reaching implications. Humans have evolved to seek meaningful patterns because it was conducive to their survival. This seems to be an enduring feature of human nature. Moreover, having a clear belief system seems to be conducive to physical and mental health. It seems likely that people will always seek meaning in life. If they are becoming less likely to find it in established religion, what might replace it? This book's final chapters address this question.

Throughout history, religion has played a crucial role in shaping civilizations and helping them survive. The following chapter discusses how religion has done this and the implications of its decline.

2

Religion Matters

This book claims that secularization has accelerated, but we do not view religion as the product of ignorance or the opium of the people. Quite the contrary, evolutionary modernization theory implies that anything that became as pervasive and survived as long as religion is probably conducive to individual or societal survival.

One reason religion spread and endured was because it encouraged norms of sharing, which were crucial to survival in an environment where there was no social security system. In bad times, one's survival might depend on how strongly these norms were inculcated in the people around you.

Religion also helped control violence. Experimental studies have examined the impact of religiosity and church attendance on violence, controlling for the effects of sociodemographic variables. Logistic regression analysis indicated that religiosity (though not church attendance) had a significant negative impact on violence after other factors were held constant (Benda & Toombs, 2000). But religion can also justify violence. Another experimental study found that aggression increased among people who had read a violent passage said to come from the Bible or an ancient scroll stating that God sanctioned the violence. The results suggest that scriptural violence sanctioned by God can increase aggression, especially among believers (Bushman et al., 2007).

Religion can shape intergroup conflict, but conflict can also shape religion. Multimethod studies reveal that the threat of warfare and intergroup tensions increases the psychological need for order and obedience to rules, which increases support for tightly regulated societies and leads people to view God as punitive (Caluori et al., 2020).

Another reason why religion spread and endured is that it is conducive to mental health and coping with insecure conditions. Virtually all of the world's major religions provide reassurance that, although a lone individual can't understand or predict what lies ahead, a higher power will ensure that things work out—in this life or the next. Both religion and secular ideologies assure people that the universe follows a plan and guarantees that if one

Religion's Sudden Decline. Ronald F. Inglehart, Oxford University Press (2021). © Oxford University Press.
DOI: 10.1093/oso/9780197547045.003.0002

follows the rules, things will turn out well. This belief reduces stress, helping people cope with anxiety and focus on dealing with the problems of survival. Without such a belief system, extreme stress tends to produce withdrawal reactions.

People under stress crave rigid, predictable rules. They need them because survival is precarious and their margin for error is slender. Conversely, people raised under secure conditions can tolerate more ambiguity and have less need for religion's absolute rules. They can more readily accept deviations from familiar patterns than people who are uncertain of survival. Living in an economically secure society with a safety net that protects people against the risks of poverty and disease brings a diminishing need for absolute rules, contributing to the decline of traditional religious institutions.

Throughout history, religion has helped people cope with insecure conditions. When they faced starvation, violence, or disease—as they very often did—religion assured them that the future was in the hands of omniscient and omnipotent gods. This faith gave people the courage to cope with threatening situations instead of falling into despair. By doing so it increased their chances of survival.

Having a firm belief system benefits both physical and mental health. A cohort study of U.S. adults found that having a strong sense of purpose in life is conducive to lower mortality rates (Alimujiang et al., 2019). Moreover, in an overwhelming majority of the countries covered by the Values Surveys, religious people tend to be happier than nonreligious people (R. F. Inglehart, 2018, pp. 164–6). This may reflect the fact that religious people tend to have a sense of purpose, a sense that things will work out despite uncertainty, and the social solidarity linked with religion's norms of sharing and charity.

A firm belief system contributes to psychological well-being, but the belief system need not be religious. Although historically religion has been the most pervasive option, other belief systems can also fill this function. When communism collapsed and the 20th century's main alternative to religion was discredited, subjective well-being fell to previously unknown levels in the former communist countries (R. F. Inglehart, 2018, pp. 158–64).

As Jared Diamond (2012, pp. 336–39) notes, evolutionary biologists believe that religion is a byproduct of features of the human brain that originally served other functions:

A plausible view is that it was a by-product of our brain's increasingly sophisticated ability to deduce cause, agency, and intent, to anticipate dangers, and thereby to formulate causal explanations of predictive value that helped us survive. We have been honed by natural selection for our brains to extract maximum information from trivial cues, and for our language to convey that information precisely, even at the inevitable risk of frequent wrong inferences.

For instance, we understand that other people have intentions like ourselves, and that individuals vary. Hence we devote much of our daily brain activity to understanding other people and to monitoring signs from them (such as their facial expressions, tone of voice, and what they do or say), in order to predict what some particular individual may do next, and to figure out how we can influence her to behave in a way that we want. Our brain's ability to discover such causal explanations is the major reason for our success as a species.

We keep trying out causal explanations. Some of our traditional explanations made the right predictions for reasons that later proved to be scientifically correct; some made the right predictions for the wrong reason . . . and some explanations made wrong predictions. For example, hunter-gatherers overgeneralize agency and extend it to other things that can move besides humans and animals, such as rivers and the sun and moon.

Diamond argues that religion itself has served seven different functions in the course of human history and that the importance of given functions vary, at different phases of development, from being extremely important to being entirely absent. These functions are:

1. Supernatural explanation.
2. Defusing anxiety through ritual.
3. Providing comfort about pain and death.
4. Standard organization.
5. Preaching political obedience.
6. Moral code of behavior toward strangers.
7. Justification of wars.

In forecasting the outlook 30 years from now, Diamond (2013, pp. 367–8) believes that if living standards continue to rise throughout the world, function 1 and functions 4 through 7 will continue to decline, but functions 2 and 3—defusing anxiety and providing comfort about pain and death—will continue to persist.

In addition to Diamond's seven functions, religion also inculcated pro-fertility norms, which were linked with societal survival under the conditions of low life expectancy and high infant mortality that prevailed throughout most of history. These conditions have declined dramatically in most countries, but because religious norms are presented as absolute, eternal commandments, they rigidly resist change.

Survival has become increasingly secure. Income and life expectancy rose and infant mortality fell from 1970 to 2010 in every region of the world (United Nations Development Program Human Development Reports, 2013). Poverty, illiteracy, and mortality are undergoing long-term decline globally (Hughes & Hillebrand, 2012; Ridley, 2011). And war, crime rates, and violence have been declining for decades (Gat, 2006; Pinker, 2011). Together with the postwar economic miracles and the emergence of the welfare state, this has produced conditions under which many people born since 1945 in Western Europe, North America, Japan, Australia, and New Zealand have grown up taking survival for granted, bringing an intergenerational shift from survival values to self-expression values. Societies no longer require high fertility rates, which have dropped dramatically. Birth control technology, labor-saving devices, and improved child care facilities make it possible for women to have children and full-time careers. Traditional pro-fertility norms are giving way to individual-choice norms concerning gender equality, divorce, abortion, and homosexuality, giving people a wider range of choice in how to live their lives.

But deep-rooted cultural norms change slowly. Virtually all major world faiths emphasize pro-fertility norms—and they do so vigorously. They present pro-fertility norms as divine edicts, violation of which will bring eternal damnation. It is necessary to make these sanctions strong because pro-fertility norms require people to suppress strong natural urges. "Thou shalt not commit adultery" goes against deep-rooted desires; requiring women to devote their lives mainly to childbearing and childrearing entails major sacrifices; and defining homosexuality as depraved and sinful imposes repression and self-hatred on gays and lesbians.

Forcing women to stay in the home and gays and lesbians to stay in the closet has high human costs, so when high human fertility rates are no longer needed, there are strong incentives to move away from pro-fertility norms—which generally means moving away from religion. As this book demonstrates, norms concerning gender equality, divorce, abortion, and homosexuality are changing rapidly. The younger birth cohorts in high-income societies are increasingly aware of the tension between religion and individual-choice norms, motivating growing numbers of them to reject religion. In the 21st century, secularization has accelerated sharply.

Religion and Economic Growth

Religion has long claimed to determine whether one attains eternal salvation or damnation, a claim that is difficult to verify empirically. But in the social sciences, the most famous claim of religion's importance is Max Weber's argument that the Protestant ethic motivated the rise of modern capitalism. His thesis gave rise to widespread controversy, with critics pointing to factual errors and questioning his argument that the causal direction ran from religious doctrine to economic behavior (Tawney, 1926).

For Weber, a central element in the rise of modernity was the move away from traditional religious authority to secular rational-legal authority, which brought a shift from inherited status to impersonal, achievement-based roles and a shift of power from society to state. Traditional value systems had to be shattered in order for modern economic development to take place.

The Confucian system was an exception in some important ways. Though (like all traditional cultures) it taught that one has a duty to be satisfied with one's station in life and to respect authority, it opened a way for social mobility through diligent study and success in the Confucian examination system. Moreover, it did not justify accepting one's place in this world by stressing the rewards this would bring in the next world or the next incarnation. It reflected a secular worldview: if one were to rise, one would do so in this world.

Apart from this, like all traditional agrarian value systems, it was geared to maintaining a stable balance in unchanging societies. Wealth mainly comes from the land, the supply of which is fixed. In this context, social mobility can be achieved only by taking someone else's land, which usually requires killing him. Consequently, agrarian value systems discourage social change in general and entrepreneurial motivation in particular, which tends to be stigmatized and restricted to pariah groups. Economic accumulation is characterized as ignoble. To facilitate the economic accumulation needed to launch industrialization, these cultural inhibitions had to be relaxed.

The Protestant Reformation helped break the grip of the medieval Christian worldview on a major part of Europe. The emergence of scientific inquiry had already begun this process, but Weber's emphasis on the role of Protestantism captures a significant factor. Prior to the Reformation, southern Europe was economically more advanced than northern Europe. During the three centuries after the Reformation, capitalism emerged, at first mainly in Protestant countries. In this cultural context, economic accumulation was no longer despised—it was taken as a sign of divine favor.

Protestant Europe manifested a remarkable economic dynamism, moving it ahead of a Catholic Europe that had previously been more prosperous. Throughout the first 150 years of the Industrial Revolution, industrial development took place mainly in the Protestant regions of Europe and the Protestant-dominated regions of the New World, and by 1940 the people of Protestant countries were on average 40 percent richer than the people of Catholic countries. Martin Luther urged people to read the Bible, and Protestantism encouraged literacy and printing, both of which inspired economic development and scientific study (Becker and Wössmann, 2009). And Protestant missionaries promoted literacy far more than Catholic missionaries did, making the historic level of Protestant missionary activity a good predictor of a country's postindependence economic performance and political stability (Trevor-Roper, 1967).

Things began to change during the second half of the 20th century, when those regions that had been most strongly influenced by the Protestant ethic began to de-emphasize economic growth—largely because they had become economically secure. By then, an entrepreneurial outlook had begun to emerge in Catholic Europe and (even more strikingly) in East Asia, which began showing higher rates of economic growth than Protestant Europe. A recent study finds that Protestant countries showed higher economic growth rates than other countries during the years from 1900 to 1930 (and probably earlier, though reliable data is not available) but not in subsequent years—in keeping with Weber's speculation that attaining prosperity might undermine the Protestant ethic (Chludzinski, 2020). This concept is outdated if taken to mean something that can exist only in Protestant countries. But Weber's broader concept, that culture influences economic growth, is an important insight.

In *The Protestant Ethic* Weber viewed religiosity as an independent variable that could influence economic outcomes. Religious beliefs affect the economy by fostering a work ethic, thrift, honesty, and interpersonal trust, which spur investment and economic growth (McCleary & Barro, 2006).

Accordingly, analyzing data from scores of countries, Barro and McCleary (2003) find that economic growth is stimulated by high rates of religious belief—but hindered by high rates of church attendance. Religious *beliefs* encourage individual traits that enhance economic performance, but higher rates of church *attendance* mean that more resources are used up by religious institutions.

Interpersonal trust is an important precondition for developing effective networks, and the Values Surveys consistently shows that the people of Protestant countries have higher levels of trust than those of countries shaped by any other religion. This remained true well into the 21st century, even in an era when few people attend church in Protestant Europe. Table 2.1 shows the results from the latest available survey from each of the 108 countries included in the Values Surveys. As it indicates, the people of Protestant Europe are much likelier to express interpersonal trust than the people of any other cultural zone. In the world as a whole, only 28 percent say that most people can be trusted. In Protestant Europe, the figure is 61 percent. The Confucian cultural zone ranks second, with 46 percent of its people saying that most people can be trusted.

Table 2.1. Percentage saying "Most people can be trusted"

Cultural Zone	%	N
Protestant Europe	61	(20,530)
Confucian	46	(7,736)
English-speaking	42	(10,533)
Baltic	31	(4,147)
Catholic Europe	28	(22,284)
South Asia	25	(10,646)
Orthodox	19	(21,321)
Islamic	18	(28,990)
Sub-Saharan Africa	15	(16,865)
Latin America	11	(17,177)
Total		*(160,229)*

Source: Latest available survey for each country in the Values Surveys.

Weber predicted that the spirit of capitalism was likely to destroy the Protestant ethic, as growing prosperity and materialism corrupted its original asceticism. And, as Niall Ferguson (2012, p. 265) points out:

> Europeans today are the idlers of the world. On average, they work less than Americans and a lot less than Asians. Thanks to protracted education and early retirement, a smaller share of Europeans are actually available for work. For example, 54 per cent of Belgians and Greeks aged over fifteen participate in the labor force, compared with 65 per cent of Americans and 74 per cent of Chinese.

Today, the Protestant ethic seems to be flourishing most strongly in East Asia. For the past 40 years, China, Hong Kong, Taiwan, South Korea, and Singapore have produced the world's highest economic growth rates. In varying degrees, they have also been importing Christianity. In South Korea and Singapore, more than 20 percent of the population is Christian. Before 1949, there were only about four million Christians in China (Miller, 2006, pp. 185–6). Today, according to official Chinese sources, there are approximately 31 million,[1] but international Christian organizations estimate that there are tens of millions more who do not publicly identify themselves because religious practice is tightly controlled by the government (Wielander, 2013, p. 3). Today there are probably more practicing Christians in China than in Western Europe. Ferguson (2011, p. 285) argues:

> Christianity is thriving in China because it offers an ethical framework to people struggling to cope with a startlingly fast social transition from communism to capitalism. . . . Just as in Protestant Europe and America in the early days of the Industrial Revolution, religious communities double as both credit networks and supply chains of creditworthy, trustworthy fellow believers."

Religion's Enduring Impact on the World's Societies

The fact that a society was historically shaped by a Protestant or Islamic or Confucian cultural heritage has an enduring impact, setting that society on a trajectory that continues to influence subsequent development even after religious institutions fade away. Thus, although few people attend church in Protestant Europe today, the societies that were historically shaped by Protestantism still show a distinctive set of values and beliefs. The same is true of historically Roman Catholic societies and historically Islamic or Orthodox or Confucian societies.

Factor analysis of data from the 43 countries covered in the 1990 Values Surveys indicates that just two dimensions—a traditional/secular-rational values dimension and a survival/self-expression values dimension—account for over half of the cross-national variance in people's responses to scores of questions.[2] Using these two dimensions, one can construct a cultural map on which the responses to many questions are boiled down to a mean score for each country, making it possible to place each country on a cultural map and to examine broad patterns of cross-cultural variation on one compact figure.

Figure 2.1 shows where each of the 43 countries surveyed around 1990 fall on this global cultural map. It sums up the cross-national differences in people's views on a wide variety of topics, including religion, politics, sexual norms, and attitudes toward work. The vertical dimension reflects the transition from agrarian societies to industrial societies, which brings secularization, bureaucratization, urbanization, and rationalization. These changes are linked with a polarization between traditional and secular-rational values. Societies whose people have traditional religious values fall toward the bottom of Figure 2.1; those with secular-rational values fall near the top. The people of traditional societies emphasize religion; they consider large families desirable and are in favor of showing more respect for authority; they rank relatively low on achievement motivation and oppose divorce, abortion, and homosexuality. The people of other societies consistently fall toward the opposite end of the spectrum on all of these orientations. The people of societies located near the top of this dimension have a secular outlook and show relatively high levels of political interest: state authority is more important for them than traditional religious authority.

Traditional values are negatively linked with a society's level of economic development but positively linked with high fertility rates. Societies with traditional values tend to emphasize maintaining the family and having many children. This is not just a matter of lip service; a society's values and its actual fertility rate are strongly correlated. This sets up a self-reinforcing process: traditional values not only inhibit norms that promote economic development; they also encourage high population growth rates that tend to offset the effects of any economic growth that *does* occur, making it still more difficult to raise per capita income. Conversely, both industrialization and

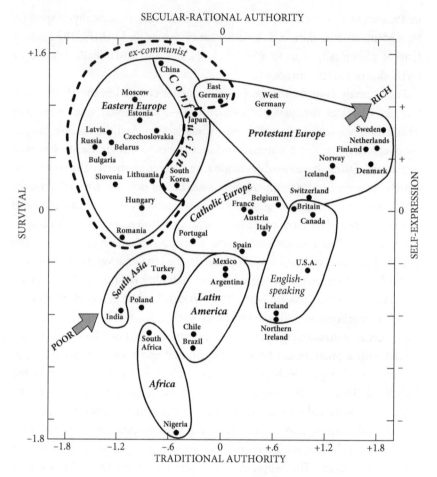

Figure 2.1 Locations of 43 societies on global cultural map, 1990–1.
Source: R. Inglehart, 1997, p. 93. Based on data from the Values Surveys.

the rise of knowledge societies are linked with declining birth rates, so the pie gets divided up among fewer people, with cultural and economic factors constituting a mutually reinforcing syndrome.

The transition from industrial society to knowledge society gives rise to another major dimension of cross-cultural variation on which a wide range of orientations are structured. The horizontal dimension of Figure 2.1 reflects the degree to which a society emphasizes survival values (toward the left of the figure) or self-expression values (toward the right). Postmaterialist values are a core component of self-expression values. Societies that emphasize self-expression values have relatively high levels of subjective well-being.

Their publics emphasize tolerance and imagination as important qualities to teach a child, rather than hard work. They support gender equality and are far more tolerant of foreigners, gays and lesbians, and other out-groups than the people of societies that emphasize survival values. Their publics have relatively high levels of support for the ecology movement. The shift from survival values to self-expression values is linked with increasing tolerance of diversity, an essential component of democracy.

As Figure 2.1 demonstrates, the 43 countries surveyed around 1990 fall into cultural clusters that reflect their historical cultural heritage, in which the historically dominant religion plays a major role. The countries of Protestant Europe form a cluster, ranking high on both the secular-rational values dimension and the self-expression values dimension. This means that the publics of Norway, Sweden, Denmark, Finland, Iceland, the Netherlands, Switzerland, and East and West Germany (two separate countries at the time of the survey) have relatively similar values in response to scores of questions. But the experience of communist rule has also left an impact: the East Germans are culturally more distant from the West Germans than the Danes are from the Norwegians, for the East Germans are also part of an ex-communist cultural zone that emphasizes both survival values and secular-rational values more strongly than most other cultures. The English-speaking countries—historically dominated by Protestantism—form another cluster; their people hold relatively similar values despite the fact that they are geographically scattered from Western Europe to North America and Australasia. The countries of Catholic Europe form another cluster, as do the (historically Catholic) countries of Latin America. The Confucian-influenced countries form yet another coherent cultural cluster that also overlaps with the ex-communist cluster. Only two African countries were included in the 1990 survey, but they too form a relatively compact cultural cluster, as do the two South Asian countries.

To take another example of the widely varying worldviews of people in different cultural zones, one of the questions linked with the traditional-secular-rational values dimension (though not used to construct it) asks, "How important is God in your life?" The responses range from 8 percent in Confucian-influenced societies to 99 percent in Muslim-majority societies, as Table 2.2 indicates. Similarly, a question linked with the survival/self-expression dimesion asks, "Do you agree that 'When jobs are scarce, men should have more right to a job than women?'" The responses vary from 5 percent agreeing that men have more right to a job than women in Protestant Europe, to 69 percent agreeing in Muslim-majority countries (see Table 2.3).

Table 2.2. Percent saying "Religion is very important in my life," by cultural zone

Cultural Zone	%
Confucian-influenced	8
Baltic	10
Protestant Europe	11
Catholic Europe	21
English-speaking	26
Orthodox	35
Latin America	54
South Asia	54
Sub-Saharan Africa	75
Muslim-majority	79

Source: Latest available survey from every country included in the Values Surveys.
Median year of survey is 2017.

Table 2.3. Percentage agreeing "When jobs are scarce, men should have more right to a job than women," by cultural zone

Cultural Zone	%
Protestant Europe	5
English-speaking	9
Baltic	17
Catholic Europe	19
Latin America	24
Orthodox	38
Sub-Saharan Africa	39
Confucian-influenced	42
South Asia	44
Muslim-majority	69

Source: Latest available survey from every country included in the Values Surveys.
Median year of survey is 2017.

At first glance these clusters might seem to reflect geographic proximity, but this holds true only when geographic proximity coincides with cultural similarity. Thus, the English-speaking zone includes the British Isles, North America, Australia, and New Zealand, while the Latin American zone extends from Tijuana to Patagonia; an Islamic subgroup within the African-Islamic cluster reflects the reality that Morocco is culturally relatively close to Indonesia, though they are almost on opposite sides of the globe. The cross-national differences found here reflect each society's economic and sociocultural history, in which a society's religious heritage plays a key role.

These two main dimensions of cross-cultural variation are attributes of societies that are fully as stable as per capita GNP. Urbanization, industrialization, rising educational levels, occupational specialization, and bureaucratization produce enduring changes in people's worldviews. They do not make all societies alike, but they do tend to make societies that have experienced them *differ* from societies that have not experienced them, in consistent ways. Consequently, although their specific religious beliefs vary immensely, the worldviews of people for whom religion is important differ from those for whom religion is not important in remarkably consistent ways. Thus, these cultural maps reflect a synthesis of enduring cultural heritage *and* major changes. This might seem contradictory, but it is not. The forces of modernization tend to move the countries that experience them upward and to the right on these cultural maps—but if all countries were moving in the same direction, at roughly the same speed, their relative positions would not change, so a cultural map from one decade would closely resemble a cultural map made two or three decades later. As a comparison of Figure 2.1 with Figure 2.2, Figures 2.3 and 2.4 demonstrate this is the case.

To a considerable extent, this is what has been happening. The publics of high-income countries have been moving upward and to the right, becoming more secular and placing greater emphasis on self-expression values. They have done so to such an extent that, in mapping the results from the later surveys, it was necessary to extend the map's boundaries to include countries that would otherwise have moved off the map. Although they are experiencing considerable change, countries' relative positions are rather stable.

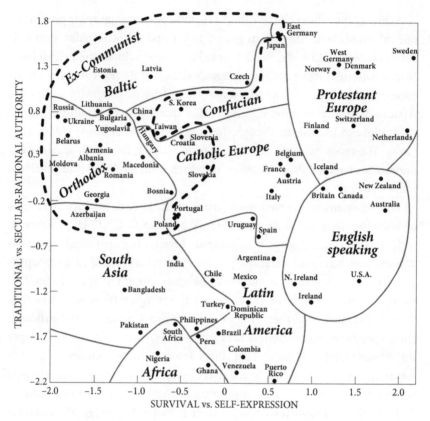

Figure 2.2 Locations of 66 societies on global cultural map, about 1995.
Source: Based on data from wave 3 of the World Values Survey and European Values Study.

Modernization: The Shift from Religious Authority to State Authority

Secularization is one of the most important aspects of modernization. This holds true despite claims that fundamentalist religion is growing throughout the world. That claim is mistaken. The apparent global rise of religious fundamentalism reflects two very different elements:

1. In the advanced industrial societies of North America, Europe, East Asia, and Australasia, traditional forms of religion have been declining *and still are*. During the past 50 years, church attendance rates have been falling and adherence to traditional norms concerning divorce,

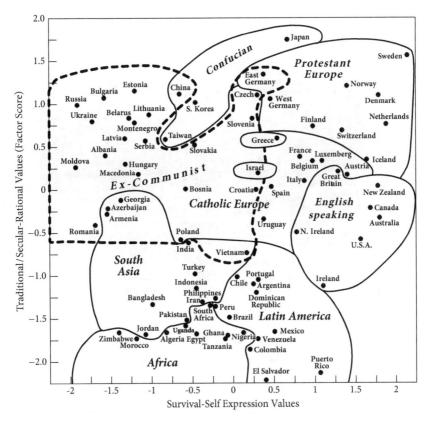

Figure 2.3 Global cultural map in 2000.

Source: Based on data from wave 4 of the World Values Survey and European Values Study.

abortion, suicide, single parenthood, and homosexuality have been eroding—and continue to erode. Resurgent fundamentalist activism has indeed been dramatic: gay bashing and the bombing of abortion centers in these countries have received widespread mass-media coverage, evoking the perception that these actions have a growing mass base. They do not. Instead, precisely because fundamentalists (accurately) perceive that their central norms are rapidly eroding, they have been galvanized into unprecedented activism. But this reflects the rearguard action of a dwindling segment of the population, not the wave of the future. Demographically, fundamentalism in these countries is in retreat, although the coronavirus pandemic could trigger a lasting major recession, stimulating the anxieties that fuel fundamentalist reactions.

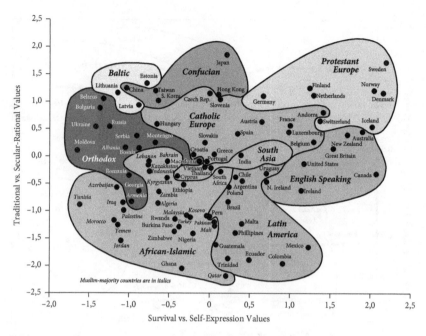

Figure 2.4 Locations of societies on the global cultural map, 2010–4.
Source: Based on data from wave 6 of the World Values Survey and European Values Study.

2. Islamic fundamentalism does have a large and stable mass constituency,
    and it has been increasingly mobilized against modernizing forces. But
    it exists in societies that have *not* modernized. Though some Muslim-
    majority societies are rich, they have not become rich by moving along
    the modernization trajectory of industrialization, occupational spe-
    cialization, rising educational levels, and rapid technological develop-
    ment, but mostly by virtue of the fact that they have large oil and gas
    reserves. Even without modernizing, it is possible to become rich if one
    has oil and gas that can be sold to industrialized countries, enabling
    traditional elites to buy the external trappings of modernization, while
    leaving most of the population behind.

    This wealth is important: it has enabled oil-rich fundamentalist
    regimes to obtain automobiles, airplanes, air conditioning, modern
    medical treatment for elites, and modern weapons. Without them, the
    fundamentalist regimes would be seen as militarily weak and techno-
    logically backward, and their mass appeal and prospects for survival
    would be weaker.

For Weber, a key component of modernization was the shift from a religiously oriented worldview to a rational-legal worldview. He emphasized the *cognitive* roots of secularization. For him, the rise of the scientific
worldview was the crucial factor that would bring the decline of the sacred/
prerational elements of religious faith. This did happen among secure and
highly educated people, but among mass publics, the rise of a sense of *security* has been an even more important factor in the decline of traditional
religious orientations. The cognitive interpretation implies that secularization is inevitable: scientific knowledge can diffuse across national boundaries rapidly, and the spread of knowledge is largely irreversible. By contrast,
a strong sense of security among mass publics emerges only after a society
has successfully industrialized, and it can be reversed by severe economic
and psychological disruption, such as that associated with the collapse of
communism. Thus, although scientific knowledge has been permeating the
world for many decades, religious fanaticism flourishes in societies that are
still in the early stages of industrialization, and fundamentalist movements
continue to emerge among the less secure strata of advanced industrial societies, especially in times of stress.

In the second half of the 20th century, the prevailing direction of change
began to shift. The origins of this shift were rooted in the economic miracles
that occurred first in Western Europe and North America, and later in
East Asia and now in South and Southeast Asia. Reinforced by the modern
welfare state's safety net, this brought unprecedentedly high levels of existential security—giving rise to cultural changes that are transforming the
economic and political systems of advanced industrial societies. The rise of
self-expression values de-emphasizes both religious and secular authority,
giving a wider range for free choice in the pursuit of individual subjective
well-being.

A core function of culture in traditional society was to maintain social co-
hesion and stability in steady-state economies. Norms of sharing were crucial to survival in an environment where there was no social security system
and no unemployment benefits; in bad times, one's survival might depend on
how strongly these norms were embraced by one's neighbors.

The key societal goal of traditional society is survival under the conditions
of a steady-state economy, in which social mobility is a zero-sum game.
During the industrialization phase, by contrast, the core societal project is
maximizing economic growth—and initially it tends to be carried out by
ruthlessly extracting the necessary capital from an impoverished populace,

regardless of the costs to the environment and the quality of life. In knowledge societies, the top priority would logically shift from maximizing economic growth to maximizing subjective well-being—which has very different implications from the goals of traditional and industrial societies.

Traditional societies vary enormously, but virtually all of them emphasize conformity to societal norms limiting violence, sexual behavior, and economic accumulation and encourage acceptance of the existing economic and social order. These norms are usually codified and legitimated within a religious framework. The shift from agrarian to industrial society brought a shift from traditional authority to rational bureaucratic authority, substituting political authority for religious authority. But in knowledge societies, authority has reached a point of diminishing acceptability. In recent decades, political leaders throughout the industrialized world have been experiencing some of the lowest levels of support ever recorded, opening the way for populist challenges. This is not simply because today's leaders are less competent than previous leaders. It reflects a systematic decline in mass support for established political institutions.

Modernization erodes some core aspects of traditional religion, such as the tendency to equate the good with the old, and the rigid rejection of social mobility and individual economic achievement. In his Protestant ethic thesis, Weber argued that this was accomplished by one type of religion replacing another. The Marxist route to modernity achieved this by replacing traditional religion with a secular ideology that initially inspired widespread hopes and expectations of a Judgment Day that would come with the Revolution. As Marxism fell into the hands of careerist bureaucrats, it lost its ability to inspire these hopes and began to crumble.

Religious orientations were central to most preindustrial societies. In the uncertain world of subsistence agriculture, the need for absolute standards and faith in an omniscient god filled major psychological needs. One of the key functions of religion was to provide a sense of certainty in an insecure environment. With modernization, people increasingly looked to the state, rather than to religion, for security.

Modernization and the Persistence of Traditional Values

My research was originally designed to examine how economic development brings cultural changes. We do indeed find that two major dimensions of cross-cultural variation are closely linked with a society's level of economic development. But even in a project originally designed to analyze the results of development, we find that countries also fall into coherent and distinctive cultural clusters that reflect each country's historical heritage and can readily be described as Protestant Europe, an English-speaking (and historically Protestant) zone, Catholic Europe, a Latin American (and historically Catholic) zone, Orthodox, Confucian, African-Islamic, and ex-communist zones. These cultural zones appear in each of the previous cultural maps (see Figures 2.3 through 2.4) and persist in the most recent one (see Figure 2.5).

Distinctive cultural zones exist, even apart from the fact that these societies have widely varying levels of economic development. The Values Surveys reveals large differences between the basic values of people in different cultural zones. These cross-cultural differences are coherent and relatively stable. And they have important behavioral consequences. The cultural variables we have examined are closely linked with a variety of important societal characteristics, ranging from the persistence and spread of stable democracy to economic growth rates and fertility rates.

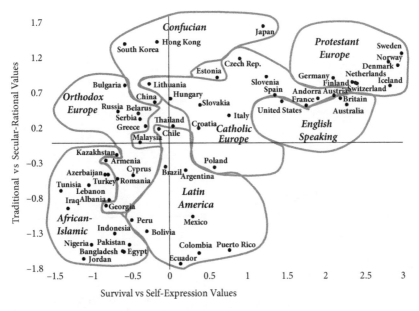

Figure 2.5 Locations of societies on the global cultural map, 2017–20.

Source: Based on data from wave 7 of the World Values Survey and European Values Study.

A given people's worldview reflects its entire historical heritage. Though the importance of economic factors is evident, a society's religious heritage has also played a major role in shaping the values, worldview, and behavior of its people today. But the role of religion seems to be declining—and that is likely to have far-reaching consequences.

3

The Secularization Debate

Well into the 20th century, leading social thinkers argued that religious beliefs reflected a prescientific worldview that would gradually fade away as scientific rationality spread throughout the world (Bruce, 1992, pp. 170–94; cf. Aldridge, 2000). A recent update of this version of secularization theory holds that the rise of science brought a cognitive shift in consciousness whereby "useful knowledge" (i.e., knowledge based on observation, experiment, and measurement) came to overshadow any other form of knowledge (Gifford, 2019). As a result, a focus on asking "useful questions" led to a growing reluctance to ask "ultimate questions." According to this view, although science has not disproven the existence of the supernatural, it has made it largely irrelevant, and Western religion has adapted to this shift by transferring its concerns from the other-worldly to the this-worldly.

To what extent is this true? Though the creationism and earth-centered cosmology of traditional religion *did* give way to evolutionary and heliocentric worldviews, this failed to discredit religion among the general public. For them, religion's main appeal proved to be more emotional than intellectual. More recently, the religious revival in former communist countries, the prominence of fundamentalist movements in Muslim-majority countries, and the rise of fundamentalist politics in Western countries have demonstrated that religion is not disappearing—and have even brought claims of a "global resurgence of religion" (Thomas, 2005).

Religious markets theory provided an influential challenge to the secularization thesis, arguing that supply-side factors such as competition between various denominations and state regulation of religion are the key influences on religious behavior (Finke & Iannaccone, 1993; Stark & Bainbridge, 1985). This school assumes that mass demand for religion is constant and cross-national differences in religious behavior simply reflect differences in what is being offered. Religious monopolies (especially state-supported ones) dampen the demand for religious products, but competitive free markets create a variety of religious products, increasing consumption by meeting a wide range of preferences. Established churches, it is argued, tend to become

Religion's Sudden Decline. Ronald F. Inglehart, Oxford University Press (2021). © Oxford University Press.
DOI: 10.1093/oso/9780197547045.003.0003

complacent monopolies, but where a free religious marketplace exists, competition between churches mobilizes church attendance: "When people have
little need or motive to work, they tend not to work, and subsidized churches
will therefore be lazy" (Finke & Stark, 2000, p. 230). Proponents of religious
markets theory argue that if the supply of churches in Europe was expanded
through disestablishment, this would bring a resurgence of religious behavior: "Faced with American-style churches, Europeans would respond as
Americans do" (Finke & Stark, 2000, pp. 237–8).

Norris and Inglehart (2004/2011) propose an alternative to both the religious markets thesis and to cognitive secularization theory, arguing that
as survival becomes more secure, the demand for religion is reduced. The
world still has many people with traditional religious views; secularization
has a strong negative impact on human fertility rates, so societies with traditional religious orientations are producing a growing share of the world's
population. Nevertheless, they argue, industrialization, growing prosperity,
and state-provided safety nets support secularization. Because these aspects
of modernization bring high levels of existential security, secularization is
spreading among the publics of virtually all high-income societies.

This version of secularization theory differs from previous versions in
several ways:

1. Instead of attributing secularization to the advance of scientific knowledge, or to modernization in general—both of which depict secularization as a universal and unidirectional process—evolutionary
   modernization theory argues that secularization largely reflects rising
   levels of existential security. Consequently, secularization is most
   likely to occur in countries that have attained high levels of security
   (and then only after a generational time lag, since it takes place largely
   through intergenerational population replacement). Secularization is
   unlikely to occur in societies where the population has not attained
   high levels of existential security, and can even move in reverse, with
   societies that experience declining existential security showing rising
   religiosity.
2. This version of secularization theory recognizes that modernization is
   path-dependent: a given country's level of religiosity reflects its specific
   historical heritage. Thus, Confucian-influenced societies were shaped
   by a secular belief system, making their starting level of religiosity relatively low—where it remains today.

3. Security is psychological as well as physical. Religion traditionally compensated for low levels of economic and physical security by providing assurance that the universe was in the hands of an infallible higher power. Similarly, Marxist ideology assured its believers that history was on their side and their cause would inevitably triumph. The collapse of the Marxist belief system left an ideological vacuum that is partly being filled by religion.

4. Though secularization normally occurs at the pace of intergenerational population replacement, it can reach a tipping point where the dominant opinion in a given milieu shifts sides, and the forces of conformism and social desirability start to favor the outlook they once opposed, producing unusually rapid cultural change. Younger and better-educated groups in most high-income countries have reached this point: instead of resisting intergenerational value change, conformism now reinforces it, accelerating the pace of change.

Defining Secularization

Secularization theory has evolved over time. Weber claimed that the scientific perspective made belief in the supernatural impossible, while Durkheim stressed the declining control of religion over society's key institutions. But both schools argued that, as people advance technologically and scientifically, they no longer need religion's magical explanations of the world (Schultz, 2006). Secularization theory flourished in the 1960s, even giving rise to claims that God is dead, but by the 1990s it was evident that religion hadn't disappeared. Growing numbers of critics claimed that the theory was false.

Whether or not secularization is occurring depends on how you define it. The first step is to define religion itself. One leading figure defines religion as "beliefs, actions and institutions predicated on the existence of gods or impersonal powers possessed of moral purpose (such as karma), which can intervene in human affairs" (Bruce, 2002, Kindle location 134). Moving on to secularization, two prominent writers define it as "the progressive autonomization of societal sectors from the domination of religious meaning and institutions" (Berger & Luckmann, 1966, p. 74). Another sees secularization as "a process of functional differentiation and emancipation of the secular spheres—primarily the state, the economy, and science—from the religious sphere, and the concomitant differentiation and specialization of religion within its own newly found religious sphere" (Casanova, 1994). Norris and Inglehart (2004/2011) argue that growing existential security tends to erode people's religious beliefs, making them attend religious services less frequently than in relatively traditional countries.

In contrast with these concepts of secularization, Stark and Bainbridge (1985, p. 430) viewed secularization theory as claiming that "the evolutionary future of religion is extinction." Defining secularization as the extinction of religion sets up an easily demolished straw man: if religion persists in any part of the world, the thesis has been refuted.

Religious markets theory, as developed by Stark and Bainbridge, became widely influential. According to them, one reason for rejecting secularization was that humans will always need religion. I would agree with this claim if it is broadened to hold that humans will always need a belief system. Humans have evolved with a deep-rooted tendency to seek patterns and explanations for the world around them and a sense of what is right and wrong. This seems to be a permanent part of human nature. But one's belief system need not be religious. Since the development of agriculture, religions have been the most common type of belief system, but Confucian-shaped civilization survived for centuries under the guidance of a secular belief system that needed no god or divine rewards, and during the 20th century, communist societies emerged and flourished under militantly secular Marxist belief systems. People were searching for meaning before today's major religions emerged and will probably continue to do so centuries from now—but they do not seem to be finding it in the same places as they did in the past. This book's final chapters address the question "What comes next?"

By the 1980s, in an era of deregulation and supply-side economics, it seemed plausible to argue that competitive free markets were best at meeting both spiritual and material needs. Moreover, communism was collapsing, and it was obvious that religion had not disappeared. Religious markets advocates claimed that religion was declining only in Western Europe—and maybe not even there. In 1992, Peter Berger—earlier one of secularization's most prominent proponents—wrote, "By the late 1970s it [secularization theory] had been falsified with a vengeance. As it turned out, the theory never had much empirical substance to begin with" (p. 15).

Another prominent critic wrote that (1) secularization theory is a hodge-podge of loosely employed ideas; (2) such secularization theory as does exist is unsupported by data after more than 20 years of research; (3) new religious movements have appeared and persisted in the most supposedly secularized societies; and (4) religion has emerged as a vital force in the world political order (Hadden, 1987).

In 1999, Rodney Stark wrote a famous epitaph for secularization theory:

> From the beginning, social scientists have celebrated the secularization thesis despite the fact that it never was consistent with empirical reality. . . . The only shred of credibility for the notion that secularization has been taking place has depended on contrasts between now and a bygone Age of Faith. . . . There have been no recent religious changes in Christendom that are consistent with the secularization thesis—not even among scientists. . . . After nearly three centuries of utterly failed prophesies and misrepresentations of both present and past, it seems time to carry the secularization doctrine to the graveyard of failed theories, and there to whisper "requiescat in pace."

The key evidence cited by those disputing any link between modernization and secularization comes from two sources: first, the fact that in one of the world's most modern nations, the United States, religious attendance was much higher than in other modern nations; second, that despite Europe's modernization, they claimed, there was "no demonstrable long term decline in European religious participation" (Stark, 1999, p. 254). According to religious markets theory, the key to flourishing religiosity was strong religious competition and little religious regulation, which forced "religious suppliers" to produce more attractive religious products (Finke & Stark, 1988; Iannaccone 1990, 1991, 1995; Stark & Bainbridge, 1987; Stark & Finke, 2000).

Many studies have tested the impact of religious competition, using the Herfindahl index of religious concentration.[1] The bulk of this research found that, contrary to religious markets' claims, there is no negative relationship between religious concentration and religious attendance. Voas et al. (2002, p. 212) concluded that "there is no compelling evidence religious pluralism has any effect on religious participation." Likewise, after reviewing the empirical studies on the role of religious pluralism, Chaves and Gorski (2001, p. 274) concluded that "the claim that religious pluralism and religious participation are generally and positively associated with one another is not supported."

Nevertheless, in 2008, Gorski and Altınordu claimed:

Outside of Western Europe, organized religion is flourishing, even resurging. So, too, is politicized religion. As the old political religions (e.g., nationalism, fascism, communism) have faded or disappeared, traditional, transcendent religion has become a key cleavage in domestic and international politics—in many contexts the key cleavage.(2008, p. 63)

In an insightful study of religion in the U.S., Putnam and Campbell (2010, pp. 74, 105) remained optimistic about the future of religion in America despite signs of decline, arguing that in some ways, religion remained as big in America as it was 40 years earlier: though church attendance had fallen, its place was being taken by new forms of religious participation such as television and internet evangelists. The U.S. unquestionably *does* have some striking religious innovations, but, as we will see, they have not staved off a massive collapse of religious belief.

In recent decades the debate between the adherents of secularization theory (Bruce, 1999, 2002; Dobbelaere, 2002; Norris & Inglehart, 2004/ 2011; D. S. Wilson, 2002) and the proponents of the religious markets model (Iannaccone 1991, 1992; Stark & Bainbridge, 1985; Stark & Finke, 2000; Stark & Iannaccone, 1994) has attracted considerable attention. But still another approach became prominent that lies between those two models: the religious individualization thesis (Davie, 2002; Hervieu-Léger, 2000; Luckmann, 1967, 1991; Roof, 1993, 2001; Wuthnow, 1998, 2010). This thesis accepts secularization theory's claim that the role of religion is shaped by industrialization, urbanization, cultural pluralization, economic growth, rising levels of economic security and education, and functional differentiation, but it sees a very different outlook for religion. While secularization theory predicts that modernization will bring about the decline in social importance of religion, the religious individualization thesis argues that modernization will change only the social forms of religion. While conceding that traditional churches and church-related behavior in modern societies have declined, the proponents of the individualization thesis contend that this does not induce diminishing individual-level religiousness. On the contrary, the decline of established religious institutions produces a *rise* of individual religiosity. The individualization thesis claims that the churches' loss of significance does not represent a loss in the relevance of religion. Individuals are freeing themselves from institutional guidelines in their religious orientations and behaviors and are increasingly making their own decisions about religion so that subjective forms of religion are replacing institutionalized forms. The proponents of the individualization thesis are relatively close to secularization theorists in seeing the reasons for religious individualization in such changes as economic growth and functional differentiation. But insofar as they reject the idea of religious decline and consider a high degree of religiosity compatible with modernity, and claim a more or less stable demand for religion, they are closer to the religious markets theorists.

Pollack and Pickel (2007) analyzed changing religiosity in East and West Germany, finding only a very slight trend toward individualization. They concluded that the dominant trend is toward secularization, and it is not reversed by religious individualization—which is only an aspect of the secularization process. This pattern is not unique to Germany. As this book demonstrates with time series data from countries containing most of the world's population, declining attendance at religious services and declining confidence in religious institutions is not being offset by growing religious belief at the individual level. On the contrary, as the following chapters demonstrate, religious *belief* is declining even more rapidly than religious *attendance*. Religious attendance persists, to some extent, even when religious belief is gone, partly in order to maintain established social contacts.

Well into the 21st century, there was no consensus that secularization was taking place. But a growing body of evidence suggested that it was—not everywhere and under all conditions, as the "extinction" definition implied, but under theoretically predictable conditions and in many places. For example, Bruce (2002) found that in 1851, between 40 and 60 percent of the adult population of Great Britain attended church on a given Sunday, but by 1998 the figure had fallen below 8 percent. Numerous other studies provide similar evidence of declining religiosity in many other postindustrial nations (Baril & Mori, 1991; Bibby, 1979; Bruce, 2002, Chapter 3; Gustafsson, 1994; Lechner, 1996; Michelat et al., 1991; Pettersson & Hamberg, 1997). To conclude, as Greeley (2003, p. xi) did, that religion is "still relatively unchanged" in the traditional Catholic nations of Europe is sharply at odds with the evidence. All the trends point consistently downward. Moreover, the erosion of religiosity is not exclusive to Western Europe; regular churchgoing has also dropped in affluent Canada and Australia (Bibby, 1979; McAllister, 1988; Mol, 1985).

The Role of Security and Economic Inequality

In 2004, Norris and Inglehart presented extensive empirical evidence from surveys in scores of countries around the world, supporting the claim that existential security is conducive to secularization. Although per capita gross national product is only a rough indicator of existential security, they demonstrated that countries with high per capita GNP show much lower levels of religious participation and religious belief than other countries—provided that their wealth is reasonably evenly distributed. Accordingly, rich countries with extensive social welfare safety nets show the lowest religiosity levels of all (Norris & Inglehart, 2004/2011, Chapter 4). This relationship between economic security and secular worldviews also exists at the individual level, as they demonstrated.

As Figure 3.1 indicates, religiosity is systematically related to individual-level incomes in postindustrial societies, where the poorest

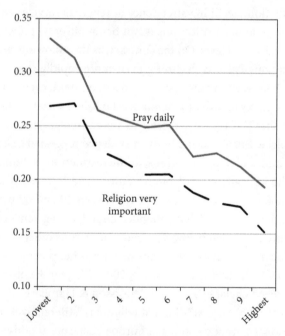

Figure 3.1 Percentage of the public who pray daily, and percentage who say that religion is very important in their lives, by household income deciles (counting all wages, salaries, pensions, and other incomes, before taxes and other deduction) in postindustrial societies.

Source: Norris and Inglehart, 2004/2011, p. 109. Based on pooled data from the 1981–2001 Values Surveys.

decile are almost twice as likely to pray daily as the richest decile, and almost twice as likely to say that religion is very important in their lives. This relationship is weaker in low-income countries, where almost everyone is highly religious: if 98 percent of the population says that religion is very important in their lives, large income-based differences are mathematically impossible. But in countries like the United States, 66 percent of the least well-off income group prayed daily, compared with 47 percent of the highest income group (Norris & Inglehart, 2004/2011, Chapter 4). Secularization is not deterministic, but it is fairly predictable if one knows a country's levels of human development and socioeconomic equality.

Norris and Inglehart (2004/2011, pp. 107–8) attributed the high levels of religiosity found in the U.S., despite its prosperity, to its high levels of inequality and weakly developed welfare system:

> Exceptionally high levels of economic insecurity are experienced by many sectors of U.S. society, despite American affluence, due to the cultural emphasis on the values of personal responsibility, individual achievement, and mistrust of big government, limiting the role of public services and the welfare state for basic matters such as healthcare covering all the working population. Despite private affluence for the well-off, many American families, even in the professional middle classes, face serious risks of loss of paid work by the main breadwinner, the dangers of sudden ill-heath without adequate private medical insurance, vulnerability to crime, as well as the problems of paying for long-term care of the elderly. Americans face greater anxieties than citizens in other advanced industrialized countries about whether they will be covered by medical insurance, whether they will be fired arbitrarily, or whether they will be forced to choose between losing their job and devoting themselves to their newborn child.[2] The entrepreneurial culture and the emphasis on personal responsibility has generated conditions of individual freedom and delivered considerable societal affluence, but one trade-off is that the United States has greater income inequality than any other advanced industrial democracy.

This is how things stood in 2004, according to Norris and Inglehart. In the intervening years, secularization began moving at a more rapid rate—for reasons linked with the current phase of modernization.

4

Evolutionary Modernization Theory
and Secularization

The degree to which people experience threats to their survival shapes their basic values (R. Inglehart, 1977, 1990 2018). Throughout most of history people lived just above starvation level, but in the years after World War II, unprecedented prosperity, extensive social welfare safety nets, and the Long Peace emerged in advanced industrial societies, launching an intergenerational shift from materialist to postmaterialist values. During the first postwar decade, this had no visible impact; 10-year-olds have little political influence. The political consequences began to be emerge only when the first postwar birth cohort reached adulthood around 1968 and student protests erupted (R. Inglehart, 1990). At that point, there was a large gap between the values of the first postwar birth cohort and all of the older cohorts, and the slogan "Don't trust anyone over 30!" made sense to the postwar generation. Student protests continued during the 1970s, though still a minority phenomenon, but by the 1980s and 1990s members of the postwar birth cohorts were occupying positions of authority. As this process continued, conformist influences reversed polarity among growing segments of the adult population of high-income countries, bringing pervasive cultural changes.

As survival becomes more secure, mass demand for religion is reduced. In the 21st century, secularization has not only persisted but accelerated in much of the world, largely because of two related cultural shifts:

1. Rising existential security brings declining demand for religion because secure people have less need for the predictability and absolute rules of traditional religion and are more open to new ideas. This has been happening for many years. But the second factor helps explain the recent acceleration of secularization.
2. All of the world's major religions encourage pro-fertility norms, which help societies replace their populations when facing high infant mortality and low life expectancy. These norms require people to suppress

Religion's Sudden Decline. Ronald F. Inglehart, Oxford University Press (2021). © Oxford University Press.
DOI: 10.1093/oso/9780197547045.003.0004

strong drives, but with low infant mortality and high life expectancy, pro-fertility norms are no longer are needed. After an intergenerational time lag, pro-fertility norms are giving way to individual-choice norms, eroding religious worldviews that had endured for centuries.

Today, developed countries' social norms are profoundly different from those of 1945. Homosexuality has gone from being criminal to being legal in virtually all high-income countries. Women have moved from being tiny minorities in the legal, academic, and medical professions and in top management to outnumbering men in some fields. And human fertility rates have moved from the high of the baby boom era to falling below the replacement level in most developed countries.

The World Values Survey and the European Values Study have monitored norms concerning sexual behavior and gender equality in successive waves of surveys from 1981 to 2020. Although deep-seated norms limiting women's roles and stigmatizing homosexuality have persisted from biblical times to the present, these surveys now show rapid changes from one wave to the next in developed countries, with growing acceptance of gender equality and of gays and lesbians and a rapid decline of religiosity.

In low-income societies, tolerance of abortion, homosexuality, and divorce is extremely low, and conformist pressures inhibit people from expressing tolerance. In Egypt, for example, fully 99 percent of the public condemned homosexuality in recent surveys—which means that even the homosexuals were saying that homosexuality was unacceptable. But intergenerational population replacement has gradually made individual-choice norms increasingly acceptable in high-income societies, initially among the student population and then among society as a whole. Among a growing share of the population, a tipping point is being reached where the prevailing outlook shifts from rejection to acceptance of new norms. As gays and lesbians come out, heterosexuals realize that people they know and like are gay, encouraging them to become more tolerant and encouraging more gays to come out (Andersen & Fetner, 2008; Inglehart & Welzel, 2005).

Religiosity and the Shift from Pro-Fertility Norms to Individual-Choice Norms

Human concepts of religion have evolved over time. The belief in a creator God concerned with moral conduct is rarely found in hunting-and-gathering societies, in which people tend to believe that local spirits inhabit and animate trees, rivers, and mountains. In premodern societies, humanity was at the mercy of inscrutable and uncontrollable natural forces. Because their causes were dimly understood, people attributed what happened to anthropomorphic spirits. The concept of a God who is concerned with human moral conduct becomes prevalent only with the emergence of agrarian societies (Nolan & Lenski, 2011, p. 72). When most people began to make their living from agriculture, they produced their own food supply but depended on things that came from heaven, like sunlight and rain. Farmers prayed for good weather, for relief from disease, and from plagues of insects.

Changing concepts of God have continued to evolve since biblical times, from a fierce tribal God who required human sacrifice and demanded genocide against outsiders, to a benevolent God whose laws applied to everyone. Prevailing moral norms have changed gradually throughout history, but in recent decades the pace of change has accelerated. The decline of xenophobia, sexism, and homophobia is part of a long-term trend away from tribal norms that excluded most of humanity, toward universal moral norms in which formerly excluded groups, such as foreigners, women, and gays, have human rights.

Many thousands of societies have existed, most of which are now extinct. Virtually all of them had high infant mortality rates and low life expectancy, making it necessary to produce large numbers of children in order to replace the population. These societies instilled a wide variety of norms, but virtually all that survived for long inculcated pro-fertility norms limiting women to the roles of daughter, wife, and mother and discouraging any sexual behavior not linked with reproduction (Nolan & Lenski, 2015). Some agrarian societies encouraged having relatively large numbers of children, while others emphasized higher investment in fewer children, but even the Western European societies that invested in fewer children produced six to eight per woman (Broadberry & O'Rourke, 2010).

In striking contrast, these societies now produce from 1.1 to 1.9 children per woman.

Not all preindustrial societies encouraged high fertility rates. From biblical times to the 20th century, some societies (such as the Shakers) advocated celibacy—but these societies have disappeared. Virtually all societies that survive today fostered gender roles and reproductive norms encouraging high fertility rates. Accordingly, the publics of every low-income and lower-middle-income country included in the Values Surveys place relatively strong emphasis on pro-fertility norms. These norms encourage women to cede leadership roles to men, becoming obedient wives who bear and raise as many children as possible, and they discourage contraception, homosexuality, abortion, divorce, and masturbation.

Throughout history and across most of the world, religion has helped people cope with survival under insecure conditions. When people faced starvation, violence, and disease—as they often did—it assured them that the future was in the hands of an omnipotent god and that if they followed his rules, things would work out. This faith gave people the courage to cope with threatening and unpredictable situations instead of falling into despair. By doing so, it increased their chances of survival.

Having a firm belief system seems to promote physical and mental health. Having a strong sense of purpose in life is linked with relatively low mortality rates (Alimujiang et al., 2019) and with relatively high levels of subjective well-being (R. F. Inglehart, 2018). One's belief system need not be religious; the crucial thing is having a firm set of convictions. Communism once provided a strong sense of meaning and purpose for many people. When this belief system eroded, and then collapsed around 1990, subjective well-being fell to previously unknown levels. The void this left has been filled by a resurgence of religion and nationalism in most ex-communist countries (including China, which, though ruled by a nominally communist party, has abandoned Marxist egalitarianism and economic principles).

In addition to establishing societal rules that reduced internal conflict, religion inculcated pro-fertility norms that were closely linked with societal survival as long as low life expectancy and high infant mortality prevailed. These conditions have disappeared in most countries, but religious norms are presented as absolute, eternal commandments, making them inherently rigid. A long time lag intervened between the point when high fertility rates were no longer needed to replace the population and the point when these changes occurred. People are reluctant to give up the norms they have always known concerning gender roles and sexual behavior, even in such societies as the U.S. Adherence to traditional norms is even stronger in less secure countries. But when a society reaches a sufficiently high level of economic and physical security that younger birth cohorts grow up taking survival for granted, it opens the way for an intergenerational shift from pro-fertility norms to individual-choice norms that encourages secularization.

The existence of a time lag between the onset of conditions that lead to deep-rooted cultural changes and the time when they transform a society means that current socioeconomic conditions don't explain current cultural changes. We are not dealing with a process in which economic growth in one year brings a corresponding increase in emphasis on individual-choice norms the next year; we are dealing with a process of intergenerational population replacement that reflects thresholds reached decades earlier.

Pro-fertility norms are a core component of most religions, so moving away from them usually entails moving away from religion. And although basic values normally change at the pace of intergenerational population replacement, the shift from pro-fertility norms to individual-choice norms has reached a point at which conformist pressures have reversed polarity and are accelerating changes they once resisted.

The intergenerational shift to individual-choice norms in Western countries has now gained enough momentum that it is unlikely to reverse itself. Though older generations feel disoriented by the rapid changes that have occurred during their lives, younger birth cohorts have grown up experiencing much higher levels of gender equality and cultural diversity than their elders did and tend to see these conditions as normal and legitimate.

Different aspects of cultural change are moving at different rates. High-income countries are currently experiencing large-scale immigration by previously unfamiliar groups and are experiencing rapidly rising inequality and declining job security, which demagogues blame on immigration. Many recent immigrants are Muslim, and hostility to them is further compounded by accounts of Islamic terrorism. Accordingly, though acceptance of gays and gender equality has risen in most developed countries, xenophobia remains widespread. Coupled with a reaction against rapid cultural change, this has enabled anti-immigrant parties to win a large share of the vote in many of these countries.

Hypotheses to Be Tested

Religion became pervasive because it helped societies survive by minimizing internal conflict and establishing rules against theft, deceit, murder, and other forms of violence; because it was conducive to mental health and encouraged solidarity and norms of sharing under conditions of existential insecurity; and because by instilling pro-fertility norms, it encouraged sufficiently high reproduction rates to replace the population. Religions played crucial roles under conditions of high infant mortality and short life expectancy. But in a growing part of the world, these conditions no longer apply. Consequently, we propose the following hypotheses:

Hypothesis 1: Historically, a coherent set of pro-fertility norms evolved that largely limits women to producing and raising as many children as possible and that stigmatizes divorce, abortion, and homosexuality and any other form of sexual behavior not linked with reproduction. Their polar opposite is a set of individual-choice norms encompassing support for gender equality and tolerance of divorce, abortion, and homosexuality. Some societies and individuals support the entire set of pro-fertility norms, while others consistently support the entire set of individual-choice norms.

Hypothesis 2: Pro-fertility norms are closely linked with religion. In societies that survive for long, these norms are supported by belief systems that impose strong sanctions—from stoning to eternal damnation—on anyone who violates them. Pro-fertility norms will be strongest in societies with strong religious beliefs; conversely, tolerance of gender equality, divorce, abortion, and homosexuality will be strongest in societies where religion is weakest.

Hypothesis 3: Support for religiosity and pro-fertility norms will be strongest in relatively insecure societies, especially those with high infant mortality rates, and weakest in relatively secure societies. Similarly, within given countries, the least secure strata will tend to support pro-fertility norms and religion, while the most secure strata will be less religious and support individual-choice norms.

Hypothesis 4: Because pro-fertility norms require people to repress strong drives, there is a built-in tension between these norms and their polar opposite, individual-choice norms. Throughout most of history, natural selection supported religion in imposing pro-fertility norms; societies that lacked these norms tended to die out. But in recent decades, a growing number of societies have attained high existential security, long life expectancy, and low infant mortality, making pro-fertility norms no longer necessary for societal survival—and opening the way for a shift from pro-fertility norms to individual-choice norms.

Hypothesis 5: Normally, there is a substantial time lag between changing objective societal conditions and cultural change. The norms one grows up with seem natural and legitimate, and abandoning them brings stress and anxiety. Consequently, deep-rooted norms usually change slowly, largely through intergenerational population replacement. Because this shift reflects the level of existential security that prevailed during the pre-adult years of people who were born decades earlier, the strongest predictor of a society's level of support for new values among the adult population will not be its current levels of life expectancy, infant mortality, and per capita GDP, but the levels that prevailed decades earlier.

Hypothesis 6: Although intergenerational population replacement involves long time lags, cultural change can reach a tipping point at which new norms come to be seen as dominant. Social desirability effects then reverse polarity: instead of retarding the changes linked with intergenerational population replacement, they accelerate them. In the shift from pro-fertility norms to individual-choice norms, this point has been reached in a growing number of settings, starting with the younger and more secure strata of high-income societies.

Throughout most of history, religious institutions (supported by the pressures of conformism) were able to impose pro-fertility norms. But the dominant causal direction can be reversed: if pro-fertility norms come to be seen as outmoded and repressive, rejection of these norms tends to bring rejection of religion. Consequently, if the hypothesized causal link between religion and pro-fertility norms exists, we should find the following patterns of cultural change:

Hypothesis 7: In societies where religion remains strong, little or no change in pro-fertility norms will take place.

Hypothesis 8: In societies where religiosity is growing, we will find growing emphasis on pro-fertility norms and declining acceptance of individual-choice norms.

Hypothesis 9: In societies where support for individual-choice norms is growing, we will find declining religiosity.

Data and Methods

We test these hypotheses against data from the WVS and the EVS (collectively, the Values Surveys). These surveys cover the full economic spectrum, including 24 low-income countries, 29 lower-middle-income countries, 20 upper-middle-income countries, and 28 high-income countries, as classified by the World Bank in 2000.[1] These surveys have been carried out in seven successive waves, from 1981 to 2020. They cover all major cultural zones, including the most populous countries in each zone, and include countries containing over 90 percent of the world's population.

Our dependent variable is religiosity, as measured by responses to the following questions:

How important is God in your life? Please use this scale to indicate. 10 means "very important" and 1 means "not at all important."

This question is a sensitive indicator of overall trends in religiosity, being the highest-loading item on the first principal component in a factor analysis of 41 questions about religion (see Inglehart, 1990, p. 183). Another measure of religiosity is:

Which, if any, of the following do you believe in?
    . . . God   Yes   No

These questions have been asked in identical form in successive waves of the Values Surveys since 1981. Detailed information concerning fieldwork, together with the questionnaires and the data from these surveys, can be downloaded from the World Values Survey site, http://www.worldvaluessurvey.org/wvs.jsp.

Although value change occurs at the individual level, we are interested in how societal-level factors lead to secularization, so many of our analyses are made at the societal level. Individual-level value change can have societal impact. It does not automatically change a society's laws and institutions, but it does make such changes increasingly likely in two ways: (1) democratic elites and institutions are necessarily responsive to mass preferences, but even autocratic leaders are not immune to them; and (2) because elites grow up and are socialized within a given society, in the long run they tend to reflect its prevailing norms.

Hypothesis 1 holds that a coherent set of pro-fertility norms exists that limits women to the role of producing and raising as many children as possible and that stigmatizes divorce, abortion, and homosexuality and any other form of sexual behavior not linked with reproduction. At the opposite pole of this dimension, we find individual-choice norms, encompassing support for gender equality and tolerance of divorce, abortion, and homosexuality.

Table 4.1 shows a country-level factor analysis demonstrating that the response to questions concerning acceptance of divorce, abortion, and homosexuality and responses to questions concerning acceptance of gender equality tend to go together. As hypothesized, the publics of some societies tend to be favorable to gender equality and relatively tolerant of divorce, abortion, and homosexuality, while the publics of other societies tend to have unfavorable attitudes toward all six topics. The factor loadings show how strongly responses to each question are correlated with an underlying pro-fertility versus individual-choice dimension. Loadings around .90 indicate that they go together in an almost one-to-one relationship. The factor scores generated by these analyses were used to create a six-item index and a three-item index of individual-choice norms. Table 4.1 shows which items were included in each of the two respective indices (which correlate at $r = .95$).

This book's analyses use the six-item index in cross-sectional analyses, but use the three-item index in time-series analyses because it provides a much

Table 4.1. Pro-fertility norms vs. individual-choice norms (principal component factor analysis)

A. Six-Item Index of Individual-Choice Norms	Factor Loading
Homosexuality is never justifiable	−.90
When jobs are scarce, men have more right to a job than women	−.89
Divorce is never justifiable	−.89
On the whole, men make better political leaders than women do	−.88
Abortion is never justifiable	−.80
A university education is more important for a boy than for a girl	−.78
B. Three-Item Index of Individual-Choice Norms	**Factor Loading**
Divorce is never justifiable	−.97
Abortion is never justifiable	−.93
Homosexuality is never justifiable	−.91

Source: National-level data from 80 countries included in the Values Surveys.
High *positive* scores indicate support for individual-choice norms.

longer time series. (Its items were included in all surveys since 1981, while the items measuring gender equality are available only since 1995.) Both indices of pro-fertility versus individual-choice norms are strongly correlated with virtually any indicator of religiosity. We will use these indices to analyze the driving forces between cultural change and secularization.

5

What's Causing Secularization?

The Rise of Individual-Choice Norms

As we have seen, publics around the world polarize along a dimension that has pro-fertility norms at one end and individual-choice norms at the other. The people of some societies consistently endorse pro-fertility norms holding that homosexuality, divorce, and abortion are never justifiable; that men have a greater right to a job than women do; that men make better political leaders than women do; and that higher education is more important for boys than for girls. Other societies consistently take the opposite stand on all six issues, endorsing individual-choice norms. The people within given societies also polarize along these lines.

Throughout most of history religion played the dominant role, successfully instilling pro-fertility norms among the population. It still plays that role in some countries, but in others the roles have recently been reversed, with changing cultural norms bringing declining religiosity. This is driven by growing rejection of the severe self-repression that pro-fertility norms impose—and by repugnance toward the sexism and intolerance that young people are increasingly likely to see in these norms. In fully 60 of the 81 countries for which time series data is available—including virtually all high-income countries—the publics have become more supportive of individual-choice norms.[1] This shift tends to bring declining religiosity. The trend is not universal: the publics of 18 countries became *less* supportive of individual-choice norms; most of them were ex-communist countries, where religiosity was rising to fill the vacuum left by the collapse of Marxist belief systems.

Most preindustrial societies encouraged high fertility rates because they faced high infant mortality and low life expectancy, making it necessary to produce large numbers of children in order to replace the population. But survival has become increasingly secure. Most societies no longer require high fertility rates, and those rates have dropped dramatically, especially in high-income societies where life expectancy has almost doubled in the past century (Prentice, 2006) and infant mortality rates have fallen to 3 percent of

Religion's Sudden Decline. Ronald F. Inglehart, Oxford University Press (2021). © Oxford University Press.
DOI: 10.1093/oso/9780197547045.003.0005

their 1950 level (Singh & van Dyck, 2010). For many years it has no longer been necessary to for women to produce six to eight children in order to replace the population. This opened the way for gradual secularization, but recently the process has accelerated sharply in many countries.

The Acceleration of Secularization in Developed Countries

We hypothesize that two factors are encouraging secularization: (1) a long-term rise in existential security and (2) a recent surge in support for individual-choice norms. This reflects the fact that rising security tends to bring a shift from pro-fertility norms to individual-choice norms. In developed countries, the long-term rise recently reached a tipping point at which support for individual-choice norms outweighs support for pro-fertility norms, causing conformist pressure to shift polarity, bringing support for norms it used to oppose and accelerating a shift that it formerly retarded.

Is this recent surge actually taking place? As Figure 5.1 demonstrates, it is—to a remarkable degree. The horizontal axis on Figure 5.1 indicates each

Figure 5.1 Shifts in support for individual-choice norms from earliest to latest survey.

Source: earliest and latest available measurement for each country in the Values Surveys.

public's level of support for individual-choice norms as measured in their country's *earliest* available Values Surveys (showing the results for all 81 countries from which two or more surveys are available over a span of at least five years). As we move from left to right, we move from pro-fertility norms toward individual-choice norms. The vertical axis shows each country's score in the most *recent* available survey, carried out from 5 to 38 years later (the median span being 22 years). As we move from low to high on the vertical axis, we move from pro-fertility norms toward individual-choice norms. These factor scores are based on pooled data from the more than 400 Values Surveys that were carried out from 1981 to 2020, for which zero is the global mean score.

The publics of Denmark, Sweden, the Netherlands, and most other high-income countries scored above the global mean in both the earliest survey and the latest available survey, so they fall in the upper right quadrant of Figure 5.1. The publics of Spain, Switzerland, the U.S., Japan, and many other countries scored below the global mean in the earliest survey but moved *above* it in the latest survey, so they fall in the upper left quadrant. The publics of Bangladesh, Pakistan, Ghana, India, Nigeria, Georgia, Colombia, and many other countries scored below the global mean on both the earliest and latest surveys, so they fall into the lower left quadrant. Three former communist countries (Albania, Serbia, and Latvia) scored *above* the global mean in their earliest survey but dropped *below* the global mean in their latest survey, so they fall into the lower right quadrant.

The dashed diagonal line indicates the cutoff between countries with rising support and those with falling support for individual-choice norms. (Countries on or near the line showed little or no change.) The publics of countries above this line showed growing support for individual-choice norms from the earliest to the latest survey, and the countries below this line showed falling support.

The publics of most countries showed rising support for individual-choice norms. To be specific, 60 countries showed rising support, 18 countries showed falling support, and 3 showed no significant change; in short, 74 percent of these publics showed rising support. As Figure 5.1 indicates, the publics of all but one of the 24 high-income countries showed rising acceptance of individual-choice norms; Greece showed no significant change, but there was a large shift toward rising acceptance in most other high-income countries. But the upward trend was not limited to high-income countries: the publics of 36 other countries also showed rising acceptance. These include seven Latin American countries and several ex-communist countries. The publics of several Muslim-majority countries moved from extremely low to slightly higher levels of acceptance, though none of the gains was large.

Fully 13 of the 18 publics that became *less* tolerant of individual-choice norms are in ex-communist countries where, we hypothesized, religiosity was spreading to fill the vacuum left by the collapse of Marxist belief systems. Though the publics of most ex-communist countries became less tolerant, the publics of nine ex-communist countries became *more* supportive of the new norms, and this includes the most prosperous ones: Slovenia, the Czech Republic, Slovakia, Poland, Hungary, Estonia, Lithuania, and Russia.

The shift from pro-fertility to individual-choice norms was strongest in high-income countries. As Figure 5.2 indicates, in the earliest available survey the publics of the 14 high-income countries ranked only slightly above the global mean for all surveys. But in the latest survey, these 14 publics showed a mean factor score of 1.9—a remarkably large shift, to a point almost two standard deviations above the global mean.

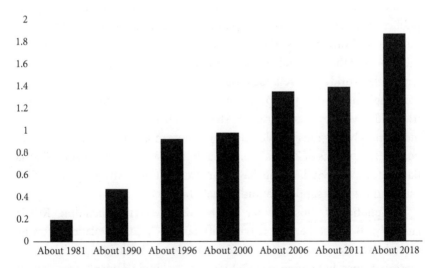

Figure 5.2 Changing support for individual-choice norms from 1981 to 2020, in pooled sample of data from 14 high-income countries. The vertical axis shows (in fractions of standard deviations) how far above the global mean (which is zero) these publics were at given time points.

To translate this shift into percentage terms: in the earliest U.S. survey, 23 percent of the American public said that divorce was never justifiable (choosing 1 on a 10-point scale); in the most recent survey, this fell to 5 percent. Similarly, in the earliest survey, 41 percent said that abortion was never justifiable; in the latest survey this fell to 22 percent. And in the earliest survey, 66 percent of the American public said that homosexuality was never justifiable; in the latest survey, only 19 percent did so. Support for gender equality moved in the same direction: in 1990, 24 percent of the U.S. public agreed with the statement "When jobs are scarce, men have more right to a job than women do"; in 2017, only 5 percent did so.

We hypothesized that secularization is largely driven by the shift from pro-fertility norms to individual-choice norms. As Figure 5.3 demonstrates, the two are closely linked: the vertical axis shows a county's relative level of religiosity and the horizontal axis shows its support for individual-choice norms. Countries whose publics rank high on pro-fertility norms tend to be strongly religious, while publics that emphasize individual-choice norms are much less religious.

Thus, the publics of Sweden, Denmark, Norway, and the Netherlands fall near the lower right corner of Figure 5.3, showing strong support for individual-choice norms and extremely low levels of religiosity. The publics of almost all high-income countries again rank high on support for individual-choice norms. Though they once were much more religious than the publics of the communist countries, today the high-income countries are among the world's least religious countries.

At the other end of the spectrum, the publics of Muslim-majority countries and low-income countries in Africa and Latin America are the world's most strongly religious people, and they adhere most strongly to pro-fertility norms. The publics of Zimbabwe, Libya, Indonesia, Yemen, Ghana, Nigeria, Bangladesh, and Saudi Arabia have extreme positions, with very high religiosity and very low support for individual-choice norms.

The publics of most former communist countries, including Russia, Hungary, Belarus, Serbia, Latvia, Lithuania, Croatia, Poland, Ukraine, Macedonia, Kazakhstan, Bosnia, Romania, and Azerbaijan, fall between these extremes, but China and Vietnam are strikingly deviant cases: though highly secular, they place little emphasis on individual-choice norms. Drawn toward secularism both by their experience under communist rule and by a secular Confucian tradition that encouraged pro-fertility norms in terms of duty to produce a male heir rather than on the basis of rewards and

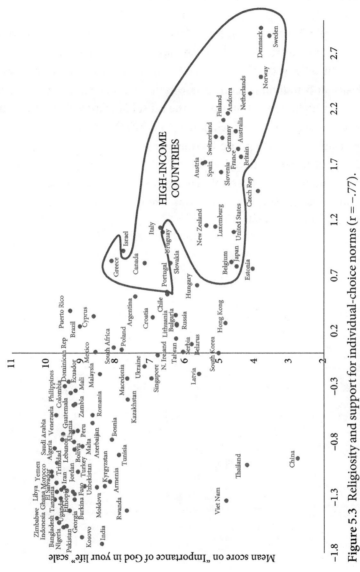

Figure 5.3 Religiosity and support for individual-choice norms (r = −.77).
Source: earliest and latest available measurement for each country in the Values Surveys.

punishments in an afterlife, they demonstrate that religion is not the only form of traditional culture that can instill pro-fertility norms. Though only marginally influenced by Confucian tradition, Thailand too is a striking anomaly. Yet despite these anomalies, the overall correlation between religiosity and individual-choice norms is a robust −.77.

As Figure 5.3 makes clear, today (though not in the past) the publics of high-income countries rank high on support for individual-choice norms and low on religiosity. The evidence is consistent with the hypothesis that religiosity and individual-choice norms have a reversible causal connection: (1) throughout most of history, the causal flow moved mainly from religion to social norms, with religion enforcing strong taboos on any sexual behavior not linked with reproduction and limiting women to reproductive roles; (2) but in recent decades, the causal flow has begun to move in the opposite direction, wichthe publics of a growing number of countries (especially high-income countries) rejecting traditional pro-fertility norms and weakening their ties to religion.

6

What's Causing Secularization?

Insecurity

Evolutionary modernization theory holds that both religiosity and pro-fertility norms are linked with existential security, and a massive body of evidence confirms this claim: religiosity and pro-fertility norms are strongest in relatively insecure societies (especially those with high infant mortality rates) and weakest in relatively secure societies. Similarly, within given countries, the least secure strata tend to favor both pro-fertility norms and religion, while the most secure strata are less religious and support individual-choice norms. Norris and Inglehart (2004/2011) presented empirical evidence supporting these claims in 2004, but subsequent research has brought significant additional support based on multilevel analyses.

Four Theories

In an important and well-designed study, Ruiter and van Tubergen (2009) tested four theories of the changing role of religion, using empirical data from 60 countries. Their findings are summarized in the following subsections.

Modernization of Ideologies

The original version of secularization theory holds that modernization leads to less religious commitment through the growth of education, science, and a technological worldview (Need & De Graaf, 1996; Weber, 1922/1993). Modernization brings rising levels of education that present a secular, empirical worldview and train people in critical thinking. This is incompatible with traditional religious worldviews, producing lower levels of religious attendance. Using multilevel logistic regression analysis, Ruiter and van Tubergen (2009) found that education has only a weak negative effect on religious

Religion's Sudden Decline. Ronald F. Inglehart, Oxford University Press (2021). © Oxford University Press.
DOI: 10.1093/oso/9780197547045.003.0006

participation at both the individual level and the societal level. This finding provides little support for the original secularization thesis; though education does seem to have a negative impact on religiosity, its impact is minor.

Modernization and Social Ties

Another version of secularization theory focuses on the diminishing strength and complexity of social ties and the decreasing tightness and homogeneity of social networks that come with urbanization. With urbanization and growing anonymity, religious communities lose control over their members, resulting in less religious commitment (Berger 1967; Durkheim 1912/1995). In rural areas, social ties between people are relatively strong, enabling the family and community to instill religion and exert social control over people's religious behavior. Ruiter and van Tubergen (2009) found that urbanization has significant negative effects on religious attendance, at both the individual and societal levels.

Modernization and Existential Security

Norris and Inglehart (2004/2011, p. 18) argue that modernization lowers people's religious belief and attendance mainly because it reduces their economic, political, and social insecurities:

> The need for religious reassurance becomes less pressing under conditions of greater security. These effects operate at both the societal level and the personal level. Greater protection and control, longevity, and health found in postindustrial nations mean that fewer people regard traditional spiritual values, beliefs, and practices as vital to their lives, or to the lives of their community.

People in prosperous modern nations face less severe economic risks and other insecurities. Although Norris and Inglehart argue that all kinds of insecurities increase religiosity, they emphasize socioeconomic inequality. In countries with relatively high inequality, the poor suffer particularly great financial insecurity, but because of heightened social and political tensions, even the rich are less secure.

Norris and Inglehart also argue that pre-adult experiences have an enduring impact on religious attendance, claiming that people who grew up during a war in their country are likely to remain more religious throughout their lives.

Ruiter and van Tubergen (2009, p. 881) find that attendance at religious services is strongly affected by the individual's own level of insecurity and that of his or her country as a whole: secure people and secure countries show the lowest levels of attendance. Income inequality proves to be the strongest predictor of religiosity: an increase in the Gini score of one standard deviation is associated with a 35 percent increase in the odds of weekly religious attendance. They also find a highly significant negative effect of social welfare expenditures on religious attendance, with a standardized effect of 26 percent.

Urbanization also shows a strong negative effect on religious attendance, with a standardized effect of 19 percent at the societal level and an 11 percent effect at the individual level. And religious regulation has a standardized effect of 17 percent by one test and 24 percent by another test. Education, on the other hand, has a standardized effect of only 3 percent. Many factors seem to have some impact on religiosity, but the variables linked with insecurity—income inequality and welfare expenditures—have the strongest effects.

Religious Markets Theory

Religious markets theory holds that state monopolies and regulation are detrimental to religion: competition between many different religious denominations brings high levels of religious participation and belief; conversely, when one religion dominates the market, religiosity fades away. Ruiter and van Tubergen (2009) conclude that there is no compelling evidence that religious pluralism has any effect on religious participation. They do find that religious *regulation* in a country substantially diminishes church attendance. This is consistent with the conservative ideology of the religious markets school but does not rescue its central claim—that free market competition between various denominations is crucial to religious participation and belief. Directly contradicting this claim, most Muslim-majority societies have one dominant religion—sometimes even imposing the death penalty for converting to another religion—but they are far more religious than the U.S. Thus, 90 to 99 percent of the populations of Egypt, Libya, and Morocco are Sunni Muslims, but these countries have some of the highest levels of religiosity in the entire world.

Ruiter and van Tubergen (2009) find some support for all four theories that they test but conclude that the evidence for the existential security thesis is strongest.

Immerzeel and van Tubergen (2011) examine the influence of various kinds of insecurity on religiosity. Using data from the European Social Surveys carried out from 2002 to 2008, they find strong support for the hypothesis that relatively high levels of insecurity, in both the past and the present, are linked with relatively high levels of church attendance. More specifically, they find that religiosity is highest among people who have an insecure job, whose parents were unemployed, whose parents had a low-status job, who have experienced a war in their own country, who have lost their partner, and who live in a country with relatively low social welfare spending or a relatively high unemployment rate.

Barro and McCleary (2006, 2019) find that economic development (as indicated by real per capita gross domestic product) has a strong negative effect on all their measures of religiosity. This applies to measures of participation, such as attendance at religious services; it also holds for measures of religious beliefs— in hell, heaven, an afterlife, or God—and for whether a person views himself or herself as religious. They find that the people of rich countries are less religious than the people of poor ones and that religiosity declines as countries get richer, but this reflects the fact that economic development is accompanied by other changes, such as the expansion of education, urbanization, and life expectancy.

Barro and McCleary (2019) also examine the effects of government intervention on religious participation and belief, finding—directly contradicting religious markets theory—that the presence of a state religion is *positively* related to all their measures of religiosity. Like Ruiter and van Tubergen, they find that *regulation* is negatively related to all measures of religiosity—which is not surprising since regulation consists of placing *limits* on religion. Viewing communist regimes as extreme cases of government regulation, designed to regulate religion out of existence, Barro and McCleary find clear negative effects from communism on all of their measures of religiosity. They find that these effects tended to dissipate over time after communism had been eliminated, but that as much as half of the negative effect remained after 10 or more years.

The Time Lag between Cultural Change and Its Causes

Now let us test the impact of various kinds of insecurity on religiosity, and also the impact of individual-choice norms. We argued that deep-rooted orientations such as religion normally change slowly, largely through in-tergenerational population replacement. Consequently, a society's level of religiosity reflects the level of existential security that prevailed during the population's pre-adult years. Thus, the strongest predictor of a society's level of religiosity will not be its *current* levels of life expectancy, infant mortality, and per capita GDP, but the levels that prevailed several decades ago.

The data in Table 6.1 supports this claim. The strongest predictor of a given society's level of religiosity is the level of existential security that it experienced several decades previously, during the adult population's for-mative years. Thus, a country's real GDP per capita in 1990 is a stronger pre-dictor of its religiosity today than is its real GDP per capita at the time of the survey.[1] Moreover, though real GDP per capita is a fairly good indicator of a society's level of existential security and religiosity, its infant mortality

Table 6.1. Correlations with "Importance of God in your life" as measured in latest available survey

Infant mortality rate in 1960	.74
Infant mortality rate in 1970	.70
Infant mortality rate in 1980	.69
Infant mortality rate in 1990	.63
Infant mortality rate in 2000	.58
Infant mortality rate in 2010	.59
Infant mortality rate in 2017	.57
Life expectancy in 1960	−.65
Life expectancy in 1970	−.64
Life expectancy in 1980	−.64
Life expectancy in 1990	−.56
Life expectancy in 2000	−.54
Life expectancy in 2010	−.58
Life expectancy in 2017	−.60
Real GDP per capita in 1990	−.64
Real GDP per capita in 2000	−.46
Real GDP per capita in 2010	−.48
Real GDP per capita in 2017	−.53

Source: World Bank reports.

rate is an even *stronger* predictor of its religiosity—in keeping with the claim that low infant mortality rates open the way for the shift from pro-fertility norms to individual-choice norms linked with secularization. Here, again, the strongest predictor of religiosity is not infant mortality at the time of the survey but the society's infant mortality rate several decades earlier, during the population's formative years. As Table 6.1 indicates, a country's infant mortality rate in 1960 has a remarkably strong correlation (r = .74) with its religiosity in 2018; the correlation between its infant mortality rate in 2017 and its religiosity in 2018 is still impressive but considerably weaker (r = .57). Consequently, the analyses that follow do not use a country's economic or demographic characteristics at the time of the survey as predictors of its religiosity; instead, we obtain the strongest explanation by using the levels that existed three or four decades earlier. One aspect of our analysis goes even farther back than that for, to a considerable extent, a country's level of religiosity today reflects its historic vulnerability to disease: the more vulnerable it was historically, the more strongly it emphasized religion and pro-fertility norms.

Murray and Schaller (2010) have developed a numerical index of the extent to which infectious diseases were historically prevalent in given countries and regions. This index is based on disease prevalence data obtained from old epidemiological atlases and is calculated for 230 countries and regions of the world. The authors hypothesize that regional variation in the prevalence of infectious diseases played an important role in the emergence of many important cross-cultural differences (Gangestad & Buss, 1993; Low, 1990), including collectivistic value systems (Fincher et al., 2008) and personality traits such as openness to outsiders (Schaller & Murray, 2008). Openness can have beneficial consequences, making people more likely to develop broad social networks, but it also comes with increased risk of exposure to socially transmitted diseases, making the costs outweigh the benefits if the prevalence of infectious diseases is high. Similarly, Fincher and his colleagues (2008) argue that collectivism, ethnocentrism, and conformism can inhibit the transmission of pathogens. Collectivism (versus individualism) is therefore relatively likely to characterize cultures that evolved historically in regions with high disease prevalence. Thornhill and his colleagues (2009) find that collectivism, autocracy, women's subordination to men, and women's sexual restrictiveness are linked with high disease prevalence; conversely, individualism, democracy, and women's rights are most widespread in countries with relatively low parasite stress.

The analyses presented in Table 6.2 show the impact of various indicators of existential security based on regression analyses in which the dependent variable is each country's mean score on our key indicator of religiosity, "How

Table 6.2. Predictors of religiosity (dependent variable is each nation's mean score on "Importance of God in your life" as measured in the latest available survey, around 2018)

Independent Variables:	Model 1	Model 2	Model 3	Model 4	Model 5	Model 6	Model 7	Model 8	Model 9
Historic disease prevalence (Murray & Schaller, 2010)	.58***	—	—	—	—	.06	—	—	—
Real GDP/capita, 1990	—	-.64***	—	—	-.31***	-.27*	—	-.09	—
Life expectancy, 1980	—	—	-.63***	—	—	—	—	—	—
Infant mortality, 1980	—	—	—	.68***	.54***	.46***	—	.28*	.29**
Individual-choice norms (6) in latest available survey	—	—	—	—	—	—	-.74***	-.46***	-.54***
Constant	7.49	9.06	16.92	5.80	5.84	6.07	7.54	7.06	6.82
Adjusted R-squared	.33	.40	.39	.45	.51	.51	.54	.58	.59
N	87	90	90	90	84	82	94	77	83

Cell entry is standardized regression coefficient.

Significance levels: * p > .05; ** p > .01, *** p > .001

Source: Attitudinal variables from 1981 to 2019 World Values Surveys and European Values Study; economic and demographic data from the World Bank, World Development Indicators.

important is God in your life?" As the results indicate, existential security is tapped by a variety of overlapping indicators, which extend far back in time.

The evidence demonstrates the enduring importance of disease prevalence: the publics of countries that were relatively vulnerable to disease in previous centuries were considerably more religious in 2018 than the publics of other countries. We hypothesized that support for religiosity and pro-fertility norms will be strongest in relatively insecure societies, especially those with high infant mortality rates, and weakest in relatively secure societies. Similarly, within given countries, the least secure strata will tend to support religion and pro-fertility norms, while the most secure strata will be less religious and support individual-choice norms.

Since disease prevalence is life-threatening, it is a strong indicator of low levels of existential security. As Table 6.2 indicates, fully 33 percent of the cross-national variation in religiosity around 2018 is predicted by the country's historic vulnerability to disease (see Model 1). Another indicator of existential security, a country's real GDP per capita, is also closely linked with religiosity: the publics of rich countries tend to be less religious than the publics of poor countries, and by itself, real GDP per capita in 1990 explains 40 percent of the cross-national variance in religiosity. Two other indicators of existential security—life expectancy in 1980 and infant mortality in 1980—are also strong predictors of religiosity, respectively accounting for 39 percent and 45 percent of the cross-national variance (Models 3 and 4). These three variables have a good deal of overlapping variance, since rich countries tend to have high life expectancy and low infant mortality. As Model 5 indicates, when we include all three as predictors of religiosity, infant mortality proves to be the strongest predictor and GDP per capita no longer has a significant independent impact. The three variables combined explain 51 percent of the cross-national variance in religiosity. Historic vulnerability to disease had a significant impact on religiosity in the early stages of history, and its influence persists through the fact that countries that were historically vulnerable to disease tend to be relatively poor and have low life expectancy and higher infant mortality today. As Model 6 indicates, these variables explain 51 percent of the cross-national variance in religiosity, but they have so much overlapping variance that historic disease prevalence no longer has a statistically significant impact on religiosity when the other two variables are taken into account.

So far, we have been examining the impact of various indicators of existential security, and as we have seen, their impact is strong. These factors are deep-rooted: historic disease prevalence reflects conditions that prevailed in previous centuries, and the other three indicators also involve substantial time lags, as is indicated by the fact that the strongest predictor of religiosity around 2018 is the society's level of infant mortality, not at the time of the survey but almost 40 years earlier, in 1980.

When we measure the impact of pro-fertility norms versus individual-choice norms, we are dealing with something that has been changing rapidly in recent years. Pro-fertility norms have been a core component of most religions since biblical times, and religious institutions were able to impose these norms for centuries. But the causal flow has begun to reverse itself, with a growing shift from pro-fertility norms to individual-choice norms bringing rejection of religion.

The six-item measure of individual-choice norms by itself explains 54 percent of the cross-national variance in religiosity (Model 7). This is a remarkably strong linkage, but it is clearly a case of reciprocal causation, with what is driving what varying over time. Additional analyses help clarify the extent to which religiosity is shaping cultural norms and the extent to which changing cultural norms are shaping religiosity. For the moment, we will simply note that there is a strong correlation between the two.

Again, our various indicators overlap considerably. High-income countries rank high on support for individual-choice norms, so when we add per capita GDP and infant mortality to the regression in Model 8, the explained variance rises to 58 percent—but the coefficient for individual-choice norms falls from –.74 to –.46, the coefficient for infant mortality falls from .68 (in Model 4) to .28, and the amount of variance explained by per capita GDP drops below statistical significance. When we drop per capita GDP from the equation (in Model 9), the coefficients for both infant mortality and individual-choice norms rise slightly. Though both historic disease prevalence and per capita GDP seem to have played important roles at earlier stages of the causal process, a society's infant mortality rate and its relative support for individual-choice norms are the key proximate predictors of religiosity in 2018—and they explain fully 59 percent of the cross-national variance. They do not explain all of the variance, leaving room for supplementary explanatory variables such as a negative reaction to religiously motivated terrorism, but we do not possess a good indicator of this variable.

In an analysis of changes over time, Zhirkov and Inglehart (2019) find that societies that ranked low on infant mortality in 1990 became less religious by 2010. Their time-series analysis indicates that existential security at time 1 predicts **change** in religiosity at time 2.

Table A.1 in the appendix shows the results of a multilevel analysis that predicts religiosity[2] on three levels: the individual, the country-year (a given country in a given year), and the country. The explanatory variables are pro-fertility norms versus individual-choice norms (using the three-item index), the time trend (measured by country-year), the log of infant mortality in 1980, and country-level dummy variables measuring the impact of the Muslim and Confucian religious traditions (as opposed to Christian traditions) and that of communist rule since World War II. To obtain comparable effect estimates, all variables were normalized to range from 0 (the smallest observed value) to 1 (the greatest observed value).

The results show the following:

1. A highly significant negative impact of individual-choice norms on religion, at the individual level: people with individual-choice norms are less religious.
2. A highly significant negative impact of individual-choice values on religion at the country-year level: societies that experience *growing* emphasis on individual-choice norms become less religious over time, but societies that experience declining emphasis on individual-choice norms become more religious over time.
3. A highly significant positive impact of time at the country-year level: countries that experience no change in emphasis on individual-choice norms become more religious over time.
4. A highly significant positive impact of infant mortality at the country level: countries with higher levels of infant mortality are more religious.
5. No significant impact of Muslim tradition on the country level: Muslim societies are just as religious as Christian societies, once individual-choice norms and human security have been accounted for.
6. A highly significant negative impact of Confucian tradition on the country level: Confucian-influenced societies are less religious than Christian societies, even after individual-choice norms and human security have been accounted for.
7. A highly significant negative impact of communist rule on the country level: postcommunist societies are less religious than other societies, even after individual-choice norms and human security have been accounted for.

These findings have clear causal implications. They support the hypotheses that growing emphasis on individual-choice norms brings declining religiosity—and conversely, that declining emphasis on individual-choice norms brings growing religiosity. The other findings do not have causal implications since they are not based on changes over time, but they do support the existential security thesis: high levels of infant mortality are linked with high levels of religiosity and vice versa.

Somewhat surprisingly, they also suggest that Muslim-majority societies are not inherently more religious than other types of countries; their high levels of religiosity can be attributed to their low levels of existential security and their strong emphasis on pro-fertility norms (though the latter may simply reflect their high levels of religiosity). On the other hand, ex-communist countries remain more secular than other societies, even after taking individual-choice norms and existential security into account. As Barro and McCready found, the negative effects of communist rule have persisted: though religiosity has been *rising* in these countries in recent decades, it still shows relatively low absolute *levels*. And Confucian-influenced societies seem to be inherently more secular than other societies; even after controlling for individual-choice norms and existential security, they show low levels of religiosity, apparently reflecting the persistence of their centuries-old heritage of having been shaped by a secular belief system.

We expect that societies with growing emphasis on individual-choice norms will become *less* religious over time, while societies with declining emphasis on individual-choice norms will become *more* religious. Moreover, our hypotheses about the changes we would expect to find in religiosity and support for individual-choice norms in different types of countries point to findings that provide valuable side information about what is causing what. For our theory postulates a strong relationship between religion and pro-fertility norms.

For most of human history, religion played the dominant role, imposing pro-fertility norms on society (as it still does in Muslim-majority societies). But recently the causal linkage has been reversed in societies where a rapid shift from pro-fertility norms to individual-choice norms is occurring. We hypothesized that (a) in societies where religion remains strong, little or no change in pro-fertility norms will take place; (b) in societies where religiosity is growing, we will find declining acceptance of individual-choice norms; and (c) in societies where support for individual-choice norms is growing rapidly, we will find declining religiosity.

Data is available from each of the three types of countries: Muslim-majority countries correspond to type a; most former communist countries fit type b; and virtually all high-income countries correspond to type c. The following chapter shows how well these predictions hold up when we examine how mass religiosity has changed over the past few decades.

7

Secularization Accelerates
in High-Income Countries

Although intergenerational population replacement involves long time lags, cultural change can reach a tipping point at which new norms become dominant. Social desirability effects then reverse polarity: instead of retarding the changes linked with intergenerational population replacement, they accelerate them, bringing rapid cultural change. In the shift from pro-fertility norms to individual-choice norms, this point has been reached in many high-income societies. When this happens, it reverses the direction of the causal flow between religiosity and individual-choice norms.

Figure 7.1 illustrates the fact that almost all high-income societies have recently reached a tipping point at which the balance shifts from the predominance of pro-fertility norms to the predominance of individual-choice norms. The vertical axis shows each country's score on a 10-point scale measuring its acceptance of divorce, homosexuality, and abortion.[1] The midpoint of this scale is 5.5. This is a rough indicator of the tipping point: lower scores indicate that the country's people predominantly support pro-fertility norms, while higher scores indicate predominant support for individual-choice norms.[2] In 1981, majorities of the publics of all of the high-income societies shown in this figure favored pro-fertility norms, with mean scores ranging from as low as 3.44 (for Spain), 3.49 (U.S.), and 3.50 (Japan) to 4.13 (West Germany) and 4.14 (Great Britain) to as high as 5.35 for Sweden, which then had the highest score of any country for which data was available. Nevertheless, even Sweden still scored below the midpoint of the scale. At that point, the public of every country in the world was predominantly favorable to pro-fertility norms—most by large margins.

But a shift toward individual-choice norms subsequently occurred among the publics of virtually all high-income countries (only nine of which are shown here; showing all of them would produce an unreadable graph).

Religion's Sudden Decline. Ronald F. Inglehart, Oxford University Press (2021). © Oxford University Press.
DOI: 10.1093/oso/9780197547045.003.0007

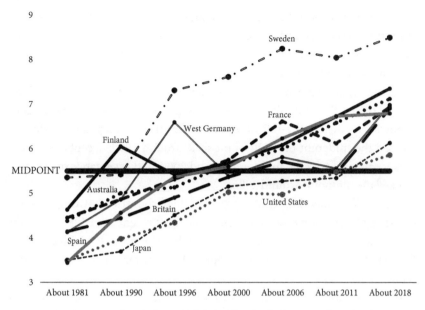

Figure 7.1 Crossing the midpoint of the individual-choice scale in high-income countries.

Source: Data from the Values Survey in given years.

Sweden remained just below the scale's midpoint in 1990, with a mean score of 5.42, and then soared to a mean score of 7.31 in 1996, moving even higher in subsequent years to reach a score of 8.49 in 2017—at which point the Swedish public had the strongest support for individual-choice norms of any country in the world. The Finnish public was still substantially below the midpoint in 1981 with a mean score of 4.63, but briefly rose to 6.05 in 1990 before retreating to 5.42 in 1996 and then rising just above the midpoint in 2000; it then continued to rise steadily, reaching a high of 7.35 in 2017. Moving more slowly, the American public remained well below the midpoint until 2011, when it almost reached the midpoint, finally rising above it in 2017 with a score of 5.86. All of these countries were well below the mean in 1981, and all of them were above it by 2019.

The Values Surveys have covered a total of 26 countries that the World Bank classified as high-income in 2000. As Table A.2 in the appendix demonstrates, the publics of all of these countries were well below the 5.50 threshold when first surveyed. Data was available from 22 high-income countries in the most recent wave of surveys (around 2018); 20 of the 22 countries had crossed the scale's midpoint by the most recent survey. The remaining two (Greece and Hong Kong) had not yet crossed the midpoint, but they had moved toward it; the same was true of all four high-income countries that were not included in the most recent wave.

As one might expect, support for each of the three components of this index crossed the midpoint at different times. Among the 14 high-income countries for which the full time series is available, acceptance of divorce crossed the midpoint of its 10-point scale around 1990; acceptance of homosexuality crossed the midpoint around 2000; and acceptance of abortion crossed the midpoint around 2006.

Support for individual-choice norms in these countries is stronger among the young than among the old. Even in the most recent available survey, the oldest cohort (born before 1933) was still below the midpoint, with a score of 5.16, but the youngest cohort (born after 1994) was far above it, with a mean score of 7.62.

In cross-national perspective, 13 of the 22 ex-communist countries for which time-series data is available showed downward trends on the individual-choice scale, and all ex-communist publics except the Czechs and Slovenes remained below the midpoint at all times for which data is available. In the latest available survey, Slovenia—the richest ex-communist country—showed the strongest support for individual-choice norms of any ex-communist country, with a mean score of 6.49, only slightly below that of Great Britain. The publics of all 18 Muslim-majority countries remained far below the midpoint at all times for which data is available, with a median score of 2.42. As hypothesized, these shifts in the balance between pro-fertility and individual-choice norms correspond closely to the shifts that took place in religiosity.

From 1981 to 2009, the publics of 14 high-income countries, including the U.S., showed a clear secularizing trend—but, as R. F. Inglehart (2018, pp. 73–4) has shown, this trend was almost entirely due to intergenerational population replacement:

> Though religiosity has remained strong in most low-income and middle-income countries, and increased in most ex-communist countries, in recent decades it has declined in almost all high-income countries—and this decline is largely due to intergenerational population replacement. Figure 7.2 shows the relationship between birth cohort and religiosity in 14 high-income countries that were surveyed in 1981 and again around

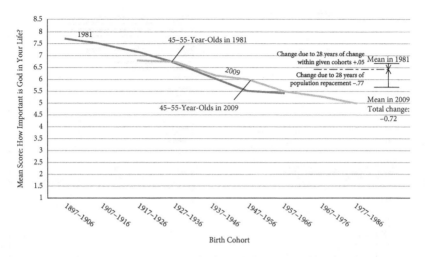

Figure 7.2 Changes in importance of religion, as measured by the question "How important is God in your life?," due to intergenerational population replacement and to within-cohort changes, in 14 high-income societies.

Source: R. F. Inglehart, 2018, p. 73. Based on combined data from EVS and WVS surveys in Australia (1981 + 2012), Belgium (1981 +2009), Canada (1981 + 2006), Denmark (1981 + 2008), France (1981 + 2008), Great Britain (1981 + 2009), Iceland (1984 + 2009), Ireland (1981 + 2008), Italy (1981 + 2009), Netherlands (1981 + 2008), Norway (1982 + 2008), Spain (1981 + 2011), Sweden (1981 + 2011), U.S. (1982 + 2011). Median span = 28 years.

2009. One line shows the 1981 levels for all cohorts, and the other line shows the 2009 levels. Both lines show a downward slope as we move from older to younger birth cohorts, reflecting the fact that younger respondents are less religious than their older compatriots. Five of these birth cohorts are present in substantial numbers in both 1981 and 2009, and their religiosity levels are almost identical at both time-points: the intergenerational differences do not reflect life-cycle effects—the religiosity of given birth cohorts remained almost unchanged across this 28-year period, so the two lines overlap where they are based on the same birth cohorts. But the 1981 line includes two highly-religious older birth cohorts (on the left side of the graph) that had dropped out of the sample by 2009. They were replaced by two much more secular younger birth cohorts (on the right side). This process of intergenerational population replacement brought a substantial decline in emphasis on religion in these 14 high-income countries, producing a net decline of .77 points on the religiosity index—a change that was almost entirely due to intergenerational population replacement.

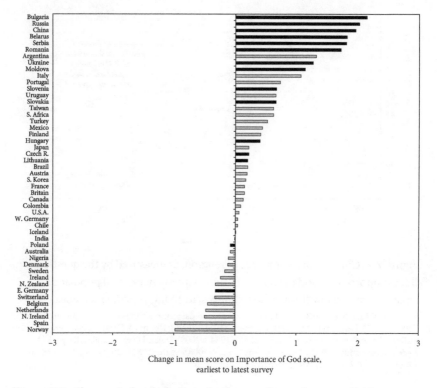

Figure 7.3 Changes in level of religiosity from earliest to latest available survey carried out from 1981 to2007 in 49 countries (ex-communist countries shown in black).

Source: Norris and Inglehart, 2011, p. 277.

But during the following years, a surge in secularization occurred that is moving much faster than intergenerational population replacement— indeed, moving so fast that it has reversed the prevailing causal flow, from one in which most publics were becoming more religious to one in which most publics are becoming more secular. The next two figures show this remarkable shift.

Not long ago, Norris and Inglehart (2004/2011) analyzed religious change in the 49 countries from which substantial time-series survey evidence was available from 1981 to 2007.[*] They found that the publics of 33 out of 49 countries had become more religious during this period; two showed

---

[*] These countries contain 60 percent of the world's population.

no significant change, and 14 became less religious. Figure 7.3 shows these findings.

In each survey, the respondents were asked to indicate how important God was in their lives by choosing a point on a 10-point scale ranging from 1, "Not at all important," to 10, "Very important." This figure compares the results from the earliest available survey with the results from the latest survey then available (around 2007). For example, the mean score of the Bulgarian public (at the top of the graph) increased from 3.56 in the earliest available survey to 5.70 in the latest survey—a gain of more than two points on the 10-point Importance of God scale. Russia rose from 4.00 in 1990 to 6.02 in 2006. China ranked very low in 1990, with a score of 1.62, but showed a large proportional gain, rising to 3.58 in 2007.

Though most of the countries on Figure 7.3 show rising religiosity, we do not find a global resurgence of religion, as a number of observers had claimed. Going against the prevailing trend, most high-income countries show *declining* emphasis on religion. Thus, from the earliest available survey to the most recent one available, in 2007, the publics of Norway, Spain, Northern Ireland, the Netherlands, Belgium, Switzerland, East Germany, New Zealand, Sweden, Denmark, and Australia all shifted toward saying that God was *less* important in their lives. But many countries do show increases, and the six largest increases are all in ex-communist countries (Bulgaria, Russia, China, Belarus, Serbia, and Romania). Overall, the publics of 13 of the 15 ex-communist countries with a substantial time series, increased their emphasis on religion. (The bars for the ex-communist countries are in black.) The severe decline of economic, physical, and psychological security that these countries experienced following the collapse of communism seems to have contributed to this resurgence of religion, as religion and nationalism moved in to fill the ideological vacuum left by the collapse of the Marxist belief system.

Marxist ideology once filled the functions of religion, providing psychological security, predictability, and a sense of purpose in life for many people. It is impossible to understand how the communist movements rose to power against severe odds, without recognizing the motivating power that Marxist ideology once had. For many decades, communism seemed to be the wave of the future, and for many people, the belief that they were building a better society gave meaning to their lives.

But ever since the 1970s, Marxist ideology had been losing credibility. Fewer and fewer people believed that communist regimes were building an ideal society that represented the wave of the future. By 1990 communism was generally discredited, and communist regimes collapsed throughout the Soviet Union and Eastern Europe. In China and Vietnam, hardline communist regimes were replaced by market-oriented regimes that were communist in name only. In the former Soviet Union and Eastern Europe, the collapse of communist regimes was accompanied by severe economic and social decline and the collapse of a belief system that had once dominated a third of the world. In China and Vietnam, nominally communist parties remained in power.

Other factors also contributed to sharply rising levels of insecurity in postcommunist societies, such as the disruption caused by the transition to market economies in the early 1990s, sharp cuts to the welfare state, rising unemployment, and falling standards of living, accompanied by rising economic inequality. Many groups lost heavily from the transition to market economies (Verhoeven et al., 2009). In Russia and most other former communist countries, per capita GDP fell sharply from 1990 until 2000.

As Figure 7.3 demonstrates, despite the overall trend toward rising religiosity from 1981 to 2007, there were mixed results. Religion became increasingly important in two types of countries: (1) less secure developing countries and (2) ex-communist societies, where the collapse of communism brought new inequalities and insecurities. But among the publics of high-income countries, the importance of religion was declining.

This book updates the analysis in Figure 7.3 with data from the most recent available surveys, carried out more than a decade later. The results show that dramatic changes have occurred since 2007 in the same 49 countries analyzed earlier. In sharp contrast with the earlier findings, which showed the dominant trend to be a *rising* emphasis on religion, the data from recent years shows an overwhelming trend toward *declining* religiosity. The public of virtually every high-income country shifted toward lower levels of religiosity, and many other countries also became less religious, including all six Latin American countries. The contrast between ex-communist countries and the rest of the world was fading, with most ex-communist countries becoming less religious. During the earlier period, from 1981 to 2007, 69 percent of the 49 publics had moved toward placing *more* importance on God, and only 31 percent moved in the opposite direction. But from 2007 to 2020, only 13 percent moved

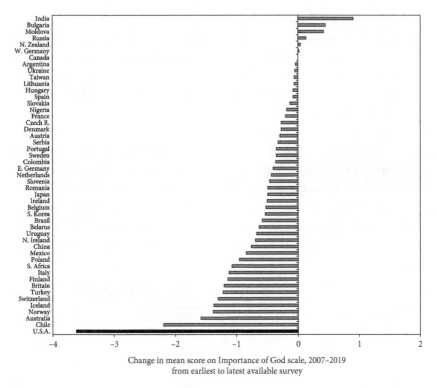

Figure 7.4 Changes in level of religiosity from earliest to latest available survey, from 2007 to 2020, in 49 countries (U.S. bar shown in black).

toward attaching more importance to God while fully 87 percent of the publics moved in the opposite direction, placing *less* emphasis on God, as Figure 7.4 shows.

From 2007 to 2020, the dominant trend reversed itself, from growing religiosity to declining religiosity. The most dramatic shift of all was found among the American public (shown in black at the bottom of Figure 7.4). In 2007, the U.S. public had shown virtually no change in religiosity since 1981, but from 2007 to 2020, the U.S. showed the largest shift *away* from religion of any country for which we have data. The United States—a highly developed country that nevertheless had high levels of religiosity—had long been cited as the crucial case demonstrating that modernization need not bring secularization. The wide variety of churches in the United States was said to maximize competition among faiths, demonstrating that where there

is competition, there will be vigorous religiosity. The U.S. still has diversity—
but since 2007 the American public has been secularizing at the most rapid
rate of any country for which data is available. Its level has fallen substantially
by virtually any measure of religiosity, and in its responses to this question
about the importance of God in one's life, it now ranks as the 11th *least* religious country in the world.

Despite the dramatic changes that occurred from 2007 to 2020, they did
not entirely erase the overall changes in religiosity that occurred during the
full period for which we have time-series data, from 1981 to 2020. Figure
7.5 shows the net changes in religiosity that have occurred during this entire period. Here, again, the ex-communist countries are shown in black.
As this figure indicates, across the full time series, there is still a major contrast between the changing levels of religiosity in ex-communist countries

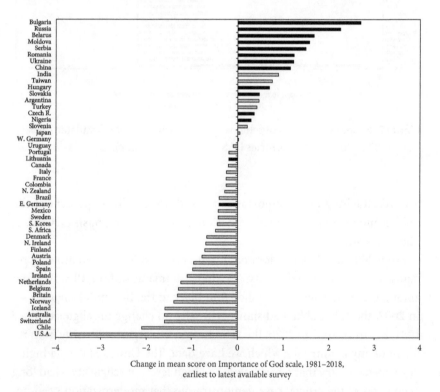

Change in mean score on Importance of God scale, 1981–2018,
earliest to latest available survey

Figure 7.5 Changes in level of religiosity from earliest to latest available survey,
1981–2020, in the same 49 countries shown in the preceding figures (ex-
communist countries shown in black).

Source: Data from the Values Surveys, 1981–2020.

and the rest of the world, with most ex-communist countries showing gains, and most other countries (including virtually all high-income countries) showing declines.

The United States: The case That Used to Disprove the Secularization Thesis

The United States—a rich country with high levels of religiosity—once constituted the crucial case supporting the claim that modernization need not bring secularization. The presence of many diverse churches in the United States, it was argued, maximized competition among faiths, demonstrating that competition brings vigorous religiosity.

The U.S. still has plenty of diversity, but it recently has been on the same secularizing trajectory as other high-income countries; indeed, since 2007 it has been secularizing at a more rapid rate than any other country for which data is available. Rising existential security and an accelerating shift from pro-fertility norms to individual-choice norms are driving a shift toward secularization in many other countries as well. Pro-fertility norms were linked with societal survival under conditions of high infant mortality and low life expectancy, but these norms are no longer needed, and after a generational time lag individual-choice norms are spreading rapidly in much of the world, contributing to a decline of religion.

In countries where the importance of God in one's life shifted in a given direction, most other indicators of religiosity also shifted in the same direction. Thus in the 1982 U.S. component of the World Values Survey, 52 percent of the American public said that God was very important in their lives, choosing "10" on a 10-point scale. In 2017 only 23 percent made this choice. Virtually all of the other indicators of religiosity also moved in this direction. In 1982, 83 percent of Americans described themselves as "a religious person." In 2017 only 55 percent did so. Conversely, while in 1982 only 16 percent of the American public said that they "never or practically never" attended religious services, in 2017 fully 35 percent said this.

In 1982, 46 percent of the American public said that they had "a great deal" of confidence in their country's religious institutions. In 2017, only 12 percent said so—a 74 percent decline. This particularly steep decline in trust in religious institutions may reflect a reaction against many prominent evangelists' open endorsement of conservative politicians—in context with the fact that 76 percent of the American public believed that churches and other houses of worship should not come out in favor of one candidate or another (Pew Research Center, November 15, 2018). In the 1960s and 1970s, mainline Christian denominations took progressive stands on major political issues, from the peace movement to the civil rights movement, without endorsing any political party. That later changed dramatically, with prominent fundamentalists becoming openly aligned with the Republican Party. As a 2020 newspaper editorial put it:

> Many Christians are deeply troubled by the inconsistency of Trump's evangelical supporters and their refusal to measure the president's behavior in office by their own ethical standards. That failure stands in sharp contrast to their reaction to Bill Clinton's moral failings. (Galli, 2020)

Evidence of declining religiosity among the American public is not limited to the Values Surveys. The General Social Survey (1972–2018) shows that the percentage of American adults who identify as Christians declined from 89 percent in 1972 to 71 percent in 2018, while the percentage who identified with no religion rose from 6 to 22 percent. Similarly, surveys carried out by the Pew Research Center show that the percentage of American adults who describe themselves as atheist, agnostic, or "nothing in particular" rose from 17 percent in 2009 to 26 percent in 2018. During

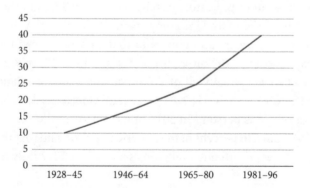

Figure 7.6 Percentage of U.S. public unaffiliated with any religion, by birth years.
Source: Pew Research Center, October 17, 2019.

that same short period, the proportion saying they attended religious services at least once or twice a month declined from 52 to 45 percent. The Pew Center surveys also found a large generation gap is religiosity; as Figure 7.6 indicates, among those born between 1928 and 1945, only 10 percent described themselves as unaffiliated with any religion in 2019, while among those born between 1981 and 1996, this figure was 40 percent (Pew Research Center, October 17, 2018).

Former communist countries continued to be the main locus of growing religiosity, as we have seen. Though from 2007 to 2020 the subjective importance of God declined in most ex-communist countries, from 1981 to 2020 only one country (Lithuania) shifted from the "growing religiosity" column to the "declining religiosity" column. But the growth of religiosity in ex-communist countries was shrinking. While in 2007 ex-communist countries constituted 13 of the 32 countries where religiosity had grown since 1981, in 2020 they constituted 12 of only 16 countries in which religiosity had grown (and all eight of the countries where it had grown most strongly).

The shifts just discussed focus on the 49 countries for which surveys covering a time span of more than 20 years is available, but if we examine the changes found in all 86 countries for which surveys covering at least five years was available in 2020, we find a similar pattern. Overall, 52 of the 86 countries show declining religiosity—but examining this more closely, we find that the publics of 26 of the 28 high-income countries became more secular, while 20 of the 25 ex-communist publics moved in the opposite direction. A clear majority of the remaining publics became more secular, including several Muslim-majority publics (though the shifts were small).

The Muslim-majority countries are a special case. The World Values Survey provides data from 10 such countries that cover a time span of at least 10 years (with a median time span of 16 years). These countries show the highest absolute levels of religiosity of any major cultural group; all of them have mean scores near the top of the 10-point scale, as Table 7.1 indicates. But they are not becoming *more* religious. (There is little room for further growth.) Moreover, although we find large religiosity differences between birth cohorts in high-income countries, age-linked differences are very small in Muslim-majority countries. Among the cohort born between 1924 and 1933, 79 percent say that God is very important in their lives (choosing "10"

Table 7.1. Changes in religiosity in 11 Muslim-majority countries providing at least 10 years of time-series data* (mean scores on 10-point Importance of God scale)

	Earliest Survey	Latest Survey
Egypt	9.63	9.96
Iraq	9.84	9.80
Jordan	9.97	9.51
Turkey	8.84	9.26
Malaysia	8.07	8.46
Azerbaijan	8.67	8.68
Morocco	9.94	9.51
Pakistan	9.88	9.53
Bangladesh	9.51	9.66
Indonesia	9.95	9.72
Mean	**9.45**	**9.45**

* Median time span is 16 years.

on the 10-point scale). Among those born between 1994 and 2003, 76 percent make that choice.[3]

Belief in God

If the United States once constituted the crucial case demonstrating that modernization needn't bring secularization, responses to the question "Do you believe in God?" played a key role in supporting this claim. Though the responses to other questions might show a secularizing trend, virtually everyone in the U.S., and overwhelming majorities in most other high-income countries, continued to say that they believed in God.

That is no longer true. Figure 7.7 shows the changing proportions saying they do not believe in God in the 14 high-income countries for which data is available from the earliest, the latest, and all or most other waves of the Values Surveys. From 1981 to 2000, the trend was flat, with about 20 percent saying they did not believe in God. It still was true that an overwhelming majority of people said they believed in God. But by 2019, the proportion

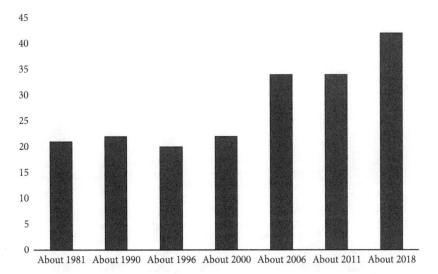

Figure 7.7 Changing percentage saying they do not believe in God in 14 high-income countries, 1981–2020.

Source: Based on pooled data from 14 high-income countries for which data is available from the earliest, latest, and all or most other waves of Values Surveys, 1981–2020. Countries are Australia, Denmark, Finland, France, Iceland, Italy, South Korea, the Netherlands, Norway, Spain, Sweden, United Kingdom, United States, and West Germany.

of nonbelievers had doubled, and among the youngest birth cohort, fully 54 percent said they do not believe in God. Here too, as with the importance of God in one's life, we find a surge of secularization.

As Figure 7.8 indicates, in 1982 only 2 percent of the American public said they did not believe in God, and as recently as 1999 only 4 percent said that. In the 2011 WVS the figure had risen to 11 percent, and in 2017 fully 22 percent of the American public said they did not believe in God—and among the youngest birth cohort, the figure was 32 percent. The trends in Figure 7.6 and Figure 7.7 move in the same direction but—though starting from a much lower base—the U.S. is changing more rapidly. In the 14 high-income countries, the proportion of nonbelievers roughly doubled from its 20th-century baseline to 2020, but in the U.S. the proportion of nonbelievers more than quadrupled.

The General Social Survey shows a similar pattern in the U.S. This survey does not ask whether the respondent believes in God, but it includes a related question, to which one response category is that the respondent "knows that God exists, with no doubts." This question was asked from 1988 to 2018. As

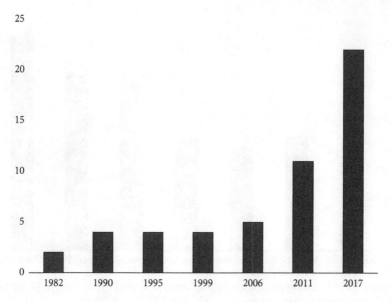

Figure 7.8 Changing percentage of the U.S. public saying they do not believe in God, 1982–2017.

Source: U.S. component of World Values Survey.

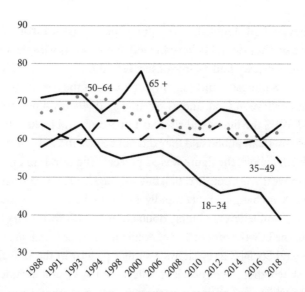

Figure 7.9 Percentage saying they "know God exists, with no doubts," by age group, 1988–2018.

Source: General Social Survey, 1972–2018.

Figure 7.9 indicates, from 1988 to 2006 the age group lines were flat, suggesting that any change in religiosity would take place gradually, as younger, less religious birth cohorts replaced older, more religious ones in the adult population. In 1988, 58 percent of the youngest age group (ages 18 to 34) said they knew that God exists, and in 2006 an almost identical 57 percent still were sure that God exists. But from that point on, this youngest age group shows a dramatic decline, with belief in God falling to 39 percent in the latest available survey, in 2018. The next older group, from 35 to 49 years of age, shows a weaker decline, from 64 percent in 2006 to 54 percent in 2018. People over 50 show still weaker declines, with those ages 50 to 64 declining from 68 percent in 2006 to 62 percent in 2018, and those over 65 declining from 66 to 64 percent. Thus, until recently, the decline was steady and gradual, moving at about the pace of intergenerational population replacement, as Norris and Inglehart had found—but since 2006, the trend has accelerated, especially among people younger than 50, and quite dramatically among those under 35.

Table 7.2 shows the mean responses of 108 publics to the question "How important is God in your life?" Responses to the latest available survey are given on a scale from 1 to 10, where 1 indicates "not at all important" and 10 indicates "very important." Once the prime example of a rich but strongly religious country, the U.S. now ranks as the 12th *least* religious of these 107 countries. Religiosity varies greatly across different types of countries. The publics of 27 countries have scores below the scale's midpoint (5.5); the names of these countries appear in boldface. All but one of them are high-income countries, Confucian-influenced countries, or ex-communist countries. The publics of 38 countries have scores above 9.0; all of these are Muslim-majority, Latin American, or African countries.

The U.S. ranks somewhat higher in response to the question "How important is religion in your life?" As Table 7.3 demonstrates, the U.S. public is the 45th least religious of the 108 publics shown here. While responses to the two questions are strongly correlated (r = −.94 at the national level and r = −.70 at the individual level), the question about the importance of God seems to tap individual beliefs more closely, while the question about the importance of religion seems to place more emphasis on the social aspects of religion and is declining more slowly than belief. In any case, the U.S. public has recently shown a declining emphasis on religion that was virtually as sharp as its declining emphasis on the importance of God. The percentage of the U.S. public saying that religion was "very important" in their lives fell from 53 percent in 1990 to 38 percent in 2017, while the percentage describing religion as "not at all important" rose from 5 to 17 percent.

Table 7.2. Importance of God in one's life, in 108 societies (mean score in latest survey on 10-point scale, where 10 = very important; countries with mean scores below the scale's midpoint are shown in boldface)

Country	Mean
China (2018)	**2.77**
Sweden (2017)	**3.56**
Denmark (2017)	**3.80**
Norway (2018)	**3.81**
Czech Republic (2017)	**3.90**
Estonia (2018)	**4.06**
Netherlands (2017)	**4.12**
Great Britain (2018)	**4.39**
France (2018)	**4.47**
Japan (2010)	**4.52**
Australia (2018)	**4.54**
U.S. (2017)	**4.60**
Belgium (2009)	**4.67**
Andorra (2018)	**4.76**
Vietnam (2006)	**4.83**
Hong Kong (2018)	**4.84**
Iceland (2017)	**4.87**
Finland (2017)	**4.89**
Germany (2017)	**4.92**
Slovenia (2017)	**4.96**
South Korea (2018)	5.04
Thailand (2018)	5.09
Switzerland (2017)	5.11
Luxembourg (2008)	5.13
New Zealand (2011)	5.39
Spain (2017)	5.42
Austria (2018)	5.49
Latvia (2008)	5.61
Hungary (2018)	5.66
Belarus (2018)	5.82
Serbia (2001)	6.07
Bulgaria (2017)	6.25
Russia (2017)	6.25
Taiwan (2012)	6.27

Table 7.2. *Continued*

Country	Mean
Lithuania (2018)	6.28
Slovakia (2017)	6.43
Chile (2018)	6.52
Portugal (2008)	6.53
Uruguay (2011)	6.65
Italy (2018)	6.72
Serbia (2018)	6.80
Northern Ireland (2008)	6.80
Croatia (2017)	6.94
Ireland (2008)	6.94
Singapore (2012)	6.98
Canada (2006)	7.17
Ukraine (2011)	7.18
Argentina (2017)	7.44
Kazakhstan (2018)	7.66
Macedonia (2008)	7.67
Rwanda (2012)	7.70
Israel (2001)	7.78
Poland (2017)	7.83
Tunisia (2019)	7.92
South Africa (2013)	8.06
Bosnia (2008)	8.12
Greece (2017)	8.12
Turkey (2012)	8.14
Armenia (2018)	8.18
Kyrgyzstan (2011)	8.33
Haiti (2016)	8.37
India (2012)	8.42
Malaysia (2018)	8.46
Moldova (2008)	8.56
Mexico (2018)	8.59
Cyprus (2011)	8.64
Azerbaijan (2018)	8.68
Romania (2018)	8.68
Uzbekistan (2011)	8.92
Malta (2008)	8.98
Kosovo (2008)	9.00

Continued

Table 7.2. *Continued*

Country	Mean
Brazil (2018)	9.04
Peru (2018)	9.11
Burkina Faso (2007)	9.11
Mali (2007)	9.17
Zambia (2007)	9.18
Ethiopia (2007)	9.21
Georgia (2018)	9.21
Lebanon (2018)	9.21
Albania (2018)	9.22
Ecuador (2018)	9.23
Bolivia (2017)	9.24
Colombia (2018)	9.31
Puerto Rico (2018)	9.32
Uganda (2001)	9.35
Dominican Rep (1996)	9.37
Iran (2007)	9.43
Nigeria (2018)	9.44
Philippines (2012)	9.48
Jordan (2018)	9.51
Pakistan (2018)	9.53
Venezuela (2000)	9.53
Algeria (2014)	9.56
Zimbabwe (2012)	9.59
Tanzania (2001)	9.61
Bangladesh (2018)	9.66
Ghana (2012)	9.67
Trinidad (2010)	9.71
Indonesia (2018)	9.72
Libya (2014)	9.72
El Salvador (1999)	9.73
Guatemala (2004)	9.73
Qatar (2010)	9.74
Saudi Arabia (2003)	9.78
Morocco (2011)	9.86
Yemen (2014)	9.87
Egypt (2018)	9.96

Table 7.3. Importance of religion in one's life, in 108 societies (mean score in latest survey in response to "How important is religion in your life?": 1 = very important, 2 = rather important, 3 = not very important, 4 = not at all important")

China (2018)	3.27
Japan (2010)	3.26
Czech Republic (2017)	3.20
Estonia (2018)	3.08
Denmark (2017)	3.00
Australia (2018)	2.98
Andorra (2018)	2.97
Netherlands (2017)	2.91
Latvia (2008)	2.90
Sweden (2017)	2.89
Switzerland (2017)	2.88
Hong Kong (2018)	2.86
Germany (2017)	2.83
France (2018)	2.82
Vietnam (2006)	2.80
Slovenia (2017)	2.79
Finland (2017)	2.78
Iceland (2017)	2.76
Spain (2017)	2.75
New Zealand (2011)	2.75
Great Britain (2018)	2.75
Norway (2018)	2.73
Uruguay (2011)	2.72
Belgium (2009)	2.72
South Korea (2018)	2.70
Luxembourg (2008)	2.69
Austria (2018)	2.66
Lithuania (2018)	2.57
Hungary (2018)	2.56
Russia (2017)	2.48
Belarus (2018)	2.42
Chile (2018)	2.39
Portugal (2008)	2.38
Taiwan (2012)	2.37

Continued

Table 7.3. *Continued*

Azerbaijan (2018)	2.37
Croatia (2017)	2.36
Slovakia (2017)	2.29
Bulgaria (2017)	2.28
Argentina (2017)	2.28
Ukraine (2011)	2.26
Northern Ireland (2008)	2.26
Canada (2006)	2.25
Ireland (2008)	2.21
Italy (2018)	2.19
U.S. (2017)	**2.18**
Kazakhstan (2018)	2.14
Albania (2018)	2.13
Serbia (2001)	2.08
Haiti (2016)	2.03
Serbia (2018)	2.01
Uzbekistan (2011)	1.98
Bosnia (2008)	1.95
Moldova (2008)	1.92
Rwanda (2012)	1.91
Poland (2017)	1.86
Singapore (2012)	1.85
Mexico (2018)	1.85
Armenia (2018)	1.83
Macedonia (2008)	1.82
Peru (2018)	1.81
Kyrgyzstan (2011)	1.80
Romania (2018)	1.77
Thailand (2018)	1.76
Turkish Cyprus (2008)	1.75
Cyprus (2011)	1.75
Brazil (2018)	1.75
Greece (2017)	1.69
Ecuador (2018)	1.68
Dominican Republic (1996)	1.67
Colombia (2018)	1.67
South Africa (2013)	1.63

Table 7.3. *Continued*

Kosovo (2008)	1.62
Bolivia (2017)	1.60
Malta (2008)	1.58
Venezuela (2000)	1.54
Puerto Rico (2018)	1.52
Turkey (2012)	1.52
Lebanon (2018)	1.46
India (2012)	1.41
Georgia (2018)	1.40
Malaysia (2018)	1.38
Uganda (2001)	1.33
Trinidad (2010)	1.31
Zambia (2007)	1.30
Iran (2007)	1.28
Ethiopia (2007)	1.27
Zimbabwe (2012)	1.22
Guatemala (2004)	1.22
Tanzania (2001)	1.20
El Salvador (1999)	1.20
Burkina Faso (2007)	1.20
Iraq (2018)	1.17
Philippines (2012)	1.16
Pakistan (2018)	1.15
Saudi Arabia (2003)	1.14
Kuwait (2014)	1.13
Morocco (2011)	1.12
Algeria (2014)	1.12
Tunisia (2019)	1.11
Mali (2007)	1.11
Ghana (2012)	1.10
Nigeria (2018)	1.08
Bangladesh (2018)	1.07
Yemen (2014)	1.06
Jordan (2018)	1.06
Libya (2014)	1.04
Egypt (2018)	1.03
Indonesia (2018)	1.02

Figure 7.10 replicates the red line on the book's front cover, showing the rise and decline of the Aggregate Religiosity Index, from 1937 to 2019. J. Tobin Grant developed this index as an indicator of the level of religious commitment, participation and activity of the American public over long periods of time, and updated it for this book (Grant, 2008). To overcome the problems of different measures and missing data in its seventeen indicators, he used a method developed by Stimson that rescales each indicator to a common scale and then estimates the underlying religiosity variable for each year despite missing data (Stimson, 1999). As this graph indicates, the religiosity of the American public was rising from 1937 to the end of the 1950s. It declined in the 1960s and 1970s and then leveled off in the 1980s and 1990s—still at a relatively high level in comparison with other high-income countries. But since

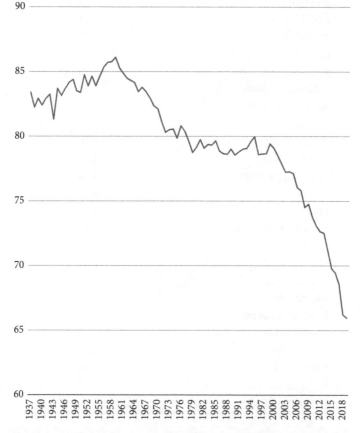

Figure 7.10 Aggregate Religiosity Index of U.S. public from 1937 to 2019.

Source: Based on 17 indicators of religiosity using a method developed by J. Tobin Grant that rescales each indicator to a common scale and then estimates the underlying religiosity variable for each year, despite missing data

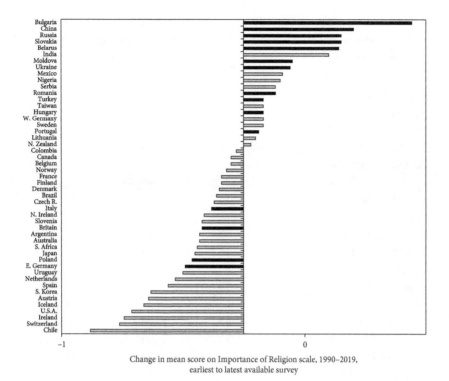

Change in mean score on Importance of Religion scale, 1990–2019,
earliest to latest available survey

Figure 7.11 Changing importance of religion in one's life, from earliest to latest available survey, 1981–2019, in the same 49 countries shown in the preceding figures, with ex-communist countries shown in black. (Polarity reversed from original coding to facilitate comparison with Figures 7.3, 7.4, and 7.5).

2000 religiosity has been declining with increasing steepness in the US—and in many other countries.

The declining subjective importance of religion was not limited to the U.S. As Figure 7.11 indicates, the importance of religion declined in 29 of the 49 countries for which a long time series is available, and the pattern resembles that found with the importance of God in one's life. The importance of religion declined in 19 of the 23 high-income countries for which data is available. Conversely, ex-communist countries once again comprise a majority of the countries where religion became subjectively *more* important, and seven of the eight countries where religion showed the greatest gains. But in four of the most prosperous and relatively secure ex-communist countries, the subjective importance of religion *declined*: Poland, Slovenia, the Czech Republic, and East Germany—all of which are now members of the European Union. Attendance at religious services shows a similar trend. Table 7.4 shows the percentage of people who say they "never or almost never" attend religious

Table 7.4. Percentage saying they "never or almost never" attend religious services (among countries for which at least a 15-year time series is available)

Country	First Survey	Last Survey	Change
Australia (1981–2018)	9	55	46
Albania (1998–2018)	7	42	35
Switzerland (1989–2017)	18	47	29
South Korea (1982–2018)	27	52	25
Azerbaijan (1997–2018)	17	41	24
Sweden (1981–2017)	27	49	22
U.S. (1982–2017)	16	35	19
Spain (1981–2017)	26	45	19
Hungary (1982–2018)	23	41	18
Argentina (1984–2017)	11	28	17
Estonia (1996–2018)	35	52	17
Belgium (1981–2009)	36	53	17
Austria (1990–2018)	17	31	14
Netherlands (1981–2017)	42	56	14
Northern Ireland (1981–2008)	12	23	13
Germany (1990–2017)	30	43	13
Egypt (2001–2018)	25	13	12
Uruguay (1996–2011)	54	66	12
Slovenia (1992–2017)	26	37	11
Canada (1982–2006)	22	32	10
Great Britain (1981–2018)	49	59	10
Ireland (1981–2008)	5	14	9
Iceland (1984–2017)	40	49	9
Mexico (1981–2018)	6	12	6
Chile (1990–2018)	20	26	6
Czech Republic (1991–2017)	54	60	6
Poland (1990–2017)	4	9	5
Peru (1996–2018)	5	10	5
Colombia (1997–2018)	9	14	5
Norway (1982–2018)	35	40	5
France (1981–2018)	59	64	5
Malta (1983–2008)	4	8	4
Croatia (1996–2017)	19	23	4
India (1990–2012)	3	6	3
Georgia (1996–2018)	14	17	3
Puerto Rico (1995–2018)	17	20	3

Table 7.4. *Continued*

Country	First Survey	Last Survey	Change
Portugal (1990–2008)	17	19	2
Indonesia (2001–2018)	1	2	1
Bangladesh (1996–2018)	1	1	0
Philippines (1996–2012)	1	1	0
Greece (1999–2017)	5	5	0
Lithuania (1997–2018)	15	15	0
Italy (1981–2018)	22	22	0
Nigeria (1990–2018)	3	1	−2
Brazil (1991–2018)	11	9	−2
Latvia (1990–2008)	31	29	−2
Romania (1993–2018)	8	5	−3
Slovakia (1990–2017)	29	25	−4
Armenia (1997–2018)	14	9	−5
Turkey (1990–2012)	32	27	−5
Finland (1981–2017)	32	26	−6
South Africa (1982–2013)	16	7	−9
Taiwan (1994–2012)	39	29	−10
Japan (1981–2010)	21	10	−11
Iraq (2004–2018)	45	33	−12
Denmark (1981–2017)	45	32	−13
China (1990)	94	80	−14
Ukraine (1996–2011)	33	17	−16
Jordan (2001–2018)	43	26	−17
Belarus (1990–2018)	54	23	−21
Russia (1990–2017)	59	36	−23
Bulgaria (1991–2017)	44	18	−26

services in all 62 countries for which a time series of at least 15 years is available. Twice as many countries show decreasing attendance as increasing attendance: 38 countries show growing percentages of nonattendance, 5 countries show no change, and 19 countries show decreasing percentages of people who never attend religious services. Belief in God and the importance of God in one's life are declining more dramatically than attendance at religious services and the importance of religion in one's life—both of which may be influenced by the desire to maintain social ties to some extent. But all indicators of religiosity are moving in the same direction.

What Caused the Recent Surge of Secularization in High-Income Countries?

Pro-fertility norms require people to suppress natural impulses, creating a powerful incentive to move to individual-choice norms. Nevertheless, throughout most of history, religious institutions, backed by natural selection, were able to impose pro-fertility norms. But a growing number of societies have now attained high levels of existential security, long life expectancy, and very low infant mortality rates, making pro-fertility norms no longer necessary for societal survival and opening the way for people to abandon those norms. In recent years the publics of most of the countries for which data is available have been shifting from pro-fertility norms to individual-choice norms.

Normally, there is a substantial time lag between changing objective conditions and cultural change. The norms one grows up with seem natural and legitimate, and abandoning them brings stress and anxiety. Consequently, deep-rooted norms usually change slowly, largely through intergenerational population replacement. But as we have seen, in high-income countries the shift from pro-fertility to individual-choice norms has reached the point where individual-choice norms become dominant, reversing the pressure of conformity. Consequently, we hypothesized (in Chapter 4) that we should find the following patterns of cultural change:

Hypothesis 7: In societies where religion remains strong, little or no change in pro-fertility norms will take place.

As we have seen, in all Muslim-majority countries for which data is available, religiosity is very strong and shows little or no change—and as Figure 5.1 demonstrated, these countries show high levels of support for pro-fertility norms and little or no change in their support for these norms.

We also hypothesized:

Hypothesis 8: In societies where religiosity is growing, we will find growing emphasis on pro-fertility norms and declining acceptance of individual-choice norms.

And as we have seen, the publics of most ex-communist countries showed steeply rising support for religion from 1981 to 2007 and (although this then slowed down) are still considerably more religious than they were in 1981. Accordingly, a majority of the ex-communist publics show rising support for pro-fertility norms over the long term, and (apart from the East Germans, who became citizens of a relatively prosperous united Germany) no ex-communist public shows a substantial movement in the opposite direction.

Finally, we hypothesized:

Hypothesis 9: In societies where support for individual-choice norms is growing, we will find declining religiosity.

As we have seen, the publics of almost all high-income countries have moved toward increasing support for individual-choice norms, showing the largest shifts among any group of countries. Accordingly, the publics of virtually all high-income countries have become increasingly secular since 2007—and in most cases these shifts are quite large.

Summary

Empirical data supports our hypotheses with minor exceptions. A coherent set of pro-fertility norms exists that limit women to the role of producing as many children as possible and that stigmatizes contraception, divorce, abortion, and homosexuality and any other form of sexual behavior not linked with reproduction. At the opposite pole, we find individual-choice norms, encompassing support for gender equality and tolerance of divorce, abortion, and homosexuality.

Support for pro-fertility norms is strongest in relatively insecure societies, especially those with high infant mortality rates, and weakest in relatively secure societies. Similarly, within given countries, the least secure strata tend to support pro-fertility norms, while the most secure strata tend to support individual-choice norms. As Table 6.2 demonstrated, existential security indicators explain 51 percent of the cross-national variance in religiosity.

Normally, there is a substantial time lag between changing objective conditions and cultural change. But cultural change can reach a tipping point where new norms become dominant, and instead of retarding the changes linked with intergenerational population replacement, social desirability effects accelerate them, bringing rapid cultural change. This point has been reached in most high-income countries. As hypothesized, the publics of almost all high-income countries have moved toward increasing support for individual-choice norms, and in most cases this shift is quite large and has accelerated.

Conversely, religiosity is very strong and shows little change in the Muslim-majority countries. Accordingly, as predicted, these countries show high levels of support for pro-fertility norms and little or no change in their support for these norms.

But, as predicted, the publics of most ex-communist countries have shown rising support for religiosity since 1981. And accordingly, a majority of these publics show rising support for pro-fertility norms.

Though early secularization theory's emphasis on cognitive factors and the religious markets school's emphasis on the role of religious entrepreneurs may have some impact, the evidence presented here suggests that emotional factors such as one's sense of existential security and the related shift from pro-fertility to individual-choice norms are considerably more important than the role of entrepreneurs or the spread of scientific knowledge. Moreover, although the United States was the key case supporting the claim that modernization need not bring secularization, since 2007 the U.S. has been secularizing even more rapidly than other high-income countries.

The most recent surveys show a surge of secularization. Many factors seem to be contributing to this. Religious fundamentalists' embrace of what young people increasingly see as reactionary policies may be driving a growing share of the younger generation away from religion. Negative reactions to highly salient terrorist acts linked with religious extremism may also contribute to the recent spread of secularization. But the evidence examined here indicates that throughout most of the world, rising security has—with an intergenerational time lag—played a pervasive role in diminishing mass demand for religion. And individual-choice norms have made a transition from minority to majority status, in many high-income countries, bringing rapidly increasing secularization.

8

What Is Replacing Religion?

People have evolved to seek patterns and explanations, and they try to put them together into a coherent belief system. This is conducive to mental health and effective coping strategies, and in societies that endure for long, political power is rarely based on naked coercion; it is also supported by a coherent legitimating myth. People need comprehensive belief systems, but religion is declining. What comes next?

We can get a sense of what is replacing religion by examining what is emerging in the countries that have moved farthest along the path from religion to individual-choice norms. And we will examine to what extent these changes seem to be functional or dysfunctional, since societies that seem to be doing well are most likely to be imitated.

The Americanization of the World or the Nordicization of the World?

Looking back at the global cultural maps starting with Figure 2.1, it's evident that the countries that rank highest on both the traditional/secular-rational dimension and the survival/self-expression dimension are Sweden, Norway, Denmark, Finland, and the Netherlands. In 1990, these countries were at the leading edge of cultural change, and these same countries (joined by Iceland in more recent surveys) continue to hold the leading position on each successive cultural map. Although many countries have been moving toward the upper right corner of the map, making it necessary to repeatedly extend the map's borders, this same group of countries has consistently led the pack.

I will refer to this group of countries as "Nordic." Although the Netherlands is not a Nordic country, its people have values similar to those of the five Nordic countries. I think it would be difficult to persuade the five Nordic peoples to adopt the label "the Greater Netherlands," so, with apologies to my Dutch friends, I'll henceforth refer to them as being part of the Nordic group—which, of course, lies within Protestant Europe.[1] Despite very low

Religion's Sudden Decline. Ronald F. Inglehart, Oxford University Press (2021). © Oxford University Press.
DOI: 10.1093/oso/9780197547045.003.0008

Table 8.1. Religiosity versus individual-choice norms factor

How important is God in your life?	−.807
Important in life: Religion*	−.770
Believe in: God	−.701
Justifiable: Homosexuality	.671
Justifiable: Divorce	.692
Justifiable: Abortion	.754

Source: Principal components factor analysis of data from latest survey of the countries included in the Values Surveys.
* This item was recoded to give it the same polarity as the other two measures of religiosity, on which low scores indicate strong religiosity.

contemporary church attendance, the people of these countries remain profoundly Protestant in many respects, sharing similar values that reflect their Protestant cultural heritage.

For many years, the U.S. was the world's richest, most powerful, and in some ways most modern country, so that when discussing modernization, people often spoke of the "Americanization" of the world. But in reality, the U.S. is not the model of where the world is moving culturally. Quite the contrary, in the cultural changes that the U.S. is currently experiencing, the American public is following a trajectory set by the Nordic publics.

We can also get a sense of likely future changes by examining the changes that accompany the shift from emphasis on religion to emphasis on individual-choice norms. As Table 8.1 demonstrates, our three top indicators of religiosity, plus the three long-term indicators of the shift from pro-fertility to individual-choice norms, define a coherent dimension, enabling us to calculate a mean score for each country, showing how far it has moved from religion to individual choice.

When we examine where each country falls on the religiosity/individual-choice dimension, as Table 8.2 does, we find that the top-ranking countries are Sweden, Denmark, the Netherlands, Norway, Iceland, and (with a slight gap) Finland. Both the global cultural maps and the countries' scores on the religiosity/individual-choice dimension suggest that the Nordic countries are at the cutting edge of cultural change. The history of major cultural changes bears this out. For example, in 1989, Denmark became the first country in the world to recognize a legal relationship for same-sex couples, establishing

Table 8.2. Rankings of each country's score on the religiosity versus individual-choice factor in the latest available survey

Sweden (2017)	1.63
Denmark (2017)	1.55
Netherlands (2017)	1.39
Norway (2018)	1.39
Iceland (2017)	1.28
Australia (2018)	1.19
Czech Republic (2017)	1.16
Andorra (2018)	1.14
Finland (2017)	1.12
Great Britain (2018)	1.12
France (2018)	1.08
Switzerland (2017)	1.05
Germany (2017)	1.03
Slovenia (2017)	0.97
Spain (2017)	0.90
Estonia (2018)	0.88
Austria (2018)	0.82
Japan (2019)	0.80
Belgium (2009)	0.71
Luxembourg (2008)	0.69
China (2018)	0.68
New Zealand (2011)	0.64
Hong Kong (2018)	0.61
United States (2017)	0.59
South Korea (2018)	0.53
Uruguay (2011)	0.48
Hungary (2018)	0.45
Slovakia (2017)	0.37
Italy (2018)	0.35
Portugal (2008)	0.25
Chile (2018)	0.24
Latvia (2008)	0.20
Lithuania (2018)	0.20
Russia (2017)	0.19
Belarus (2018)	0.16
Taiwan (2012)	0.14
Bulgaria (2017)	0.13

Continued

Table 8.2. *Continued*

Croatia (2017)	0.12
Argentina (2017)	0.11
Thailand (2013)	0.08
Ireland (2008)	0.03
Greece (2017)	0.00
Ukraine (2011)	−0.05
Northern Ireland (2008)	−0.07
Singapore (2012)	−0.10
Poland (2017)	−0.18
Cyprus (2011)	−0.20
Kazakhstan (2018)	−0.23
Mexico (2018)	−0.23
Haiti (2016)	−0.24
South Africa (2013)	−0.24
Brazil (2018)	−0.25
Puerto Rico (2018)	−0.26
Macedonia (2008)	−0.33
Azerbaijan (2018)	−0.37
Malaysia (2018)	−0.39
Bosnia (2008)	−0.45
Colombia (2018)	−0.45
Ecuador (2018)	−0.49
Romania (2018)	−0.49
Albania (2018)	−0.50
Turkish Cyprus (2008)	−0.53
Peru (2018)	−0.53
Armenia (2018)	−0.55
Philippines (2012)	−0.56
Bolivia (2017)	−0.57
Kyrgyzstan (2011)	−0.60
Malta (2008)	−0.60
Rwanda (2012)	−0.60
Uzbekistan (2011)	−0.63
Moldova (2008)	−0.64
Lebanon (2018)	−0.67
Tunisia (2019)	−0.67
Turkey (2018)	−0.77
Algeria (2014)	−0.78
Trinidad (2010)	−0.79

Table 8.2. *Continued*

Georgia (2018)	−0.81
Saudi Arabia (2003)	−0.81
India (2012)	−0.86
Zimbabwe (2012)	−0.86
El Salvador (1999)	−0.87
Uganda (2001)	−0.88
Jordan (2018)	−0.89
Morocco (2011)	−0.89
Tanzania (2001)	−0.91
Libya (2014)	−0.92
Nigeria (2018)	−0.97
Pakistan (2018)	**−0.97**
Bangladesh (2018)	**−0.98**
Indonesia (2018)	**−0.98**

Source: Data from latest available survey for countries included in Waves 6 or 7 of the Values Surveys.

registered partnerships. In 2001, the Netherlands moved a step farther, becoming the first country to legalize same-sex marriage—and it was soon followed by Belgium (2003), Spain (20005), Canada (2005), South Africa (2006), Norway (2009), Sweden (2009), Portugal (2010), Iceland (2010), Argentina (2010), Denmark (2012), Brazil (2013), France (2013), Uruguay (2013), New Zealand (2013), Luxembourg (2015), the United States (2015), and a growing number of other countries.

The Nordic Synthesis: The Protestant Ethic Meets the Welfare State

The Nordic countries seem to be at the cutting edge of cultural change, and their distinctive character seems to reflect a synthesis between the Protestant ethic and the welfare state. As chapter 2 demonstrated, Protestantism left an enduring imprint on the people who were shaped by it. But the Social Democratic welfare state that emerged in the Nordic countries in the 20th century modified this heritage by providing universal health coverage; high levels of state support for education, extensive welfare spending, child care, and pensions; and an ethos of social solidarity. These countries are also char-acterized by rapidly declining religiosity.

Is this good or bad? More specifically, does declining religiosity produce societies of self-indulgent, amoral nihilists? That doesn't seem to be the case. Let's examine the distinctive characteristics of the Nordic countries in detail.

Piketty (2014) has analyzed the evolution of income inequality in the U.S., Britain, Germany, France, and Sweden from 1900 to 2010, demonstrating that at the start of the 20th century all four European countries had higher levels of income inequality than the U.S.[2] Sweden is distinctive: though in the early 20th century it had considerably higher levels of inequality than the U.S., by the 1920s it had attained a substantially lower level of ine-quality than all four other countries—and has maintained that distinction to the present. In 2010, the top decile in the U.S. got almost 50 percent of the total income, while in Sweden it got only 28 percent. The advanced welfare state culture introduced by Sweden's long-dominant Social Democrats| has persisted to the present despite subsequent alternation in power with con-servative parties. Social Democratic policies were also adopted by the other Nordic countries, which became increasingly secure and egalitarian socie-ties. Despite their declining emphasis on religion, they are characterized by high levels of interpersonal trust, tolerance, honesty, social solidarity, punc-tuality, gender equality, and commitment to democratic norms. And while their Social Democratic policies brought substantial reallocation of wealth, this did not impoverish them. On the contrary, as Table 8.3 demonstrates, the Nordic countries now rank among the world's healthiest, best educated, and most prosperous countries. In the long run, investment in education, health care, child care, and social security seem to pay off.

There has been an erosion of traditional religious morality in the Nordic countries, but the emerging culture has a clear morality of its own. Divorce is no longer stigmatized as sinful, but the sexual harassment of women, which most societies once ignored or tacitly accepted, has become so-cially unacceptable in these countries, becoming as much a sin as divorce once was. Moreover, according to Transparency International (2019), the Nordic countries have some of the least corrupt governments in the world. They also practice Christian charity, spending a larger share of their na-tional income on foreign aid than most other countries, and they obey the Fifth Commandment, having exceptionally low murder rates. This chapter explores the nature of the Nordic synthesis in some detail, finding that these countries lead the world in many important respects.

Table 8.3. UN Human Development rankings in 2018

	Life Expectancy	Expected Years of Schooling	GDP/Capita (PPP $)
1 Norway	82.3	18.1	$68,059
2 Switzerland	83.6	16.2	59,375
3 Ireland	82.1	18.8	55,660
4 Germany	81.2	17.1	46,946
5 Hong Kong	84.7	16.5	60,221
6 Australia	83.3	22.1	44,097
7 Iceland	82.9	19.2	47,566
8 Sweden	82.7	18.8	47,958
9 Singapore	83.5	16.2	83,793
10 Netherlands	82.1	18.0	50,013
11 Denmark	80.8	19.1	48,836
12 Finland	81.7	19.3	41,779
13 Canada	82.3	16.1	43,602
14 New Zealand	82.1	18.8	35,108
15 United Kingdom	81.2	17.4	39,507
16 United States	78.9	16.3	56,140
17 Belgium	81.5	19.7	43,821
18 Liechtenstein	80.5	14.7	99,732
19 Japan	84.5	15.2	40,799
20 Austria	81.4	16.3	46,231
107 Libya	72.7	12.8	11,685
111 Indonesia	71.5	12.9	11,256
135 Bangladesh	72.3	11.2	4,057
152 Pakistan	67.1	8.5	5,190
158 Nigeria	54.3	9.7	5,086

Source: United Nations Development Program Human Development Reports, 2019.

Having been born in, spent most of my life in, and raised children in the United States, it is my favorite country. By many criteria, it ranks as one of the best countries in the world. But having lived in other countries for extended periods of time, I'm aware that some of them are just as livable as the U.S.—and a rich array of statistical evidence from the UN, the World Bank, the World Health Organization, Transparency International, Freedom House, the Varieties of Democracy Institute, and other international organizations suggests that today some of them are functioning even better than the U.S. As we'll shortly demonstrate, this is particularly true of the Nordic group, whose members rank high or lead the world on a wide range of important attributes.

Let's start with the UN Human Development rankings. As Table 8.3 indicates, the Nordic countries include 6 of the 12 top-ranking countries among the 189 countries that are ranked. Conversely, the five countries that rank at the opposite end on the religiosity/individual-choice factor shown on Table 8.2 rank from 107th to 158th on the Human Development scale. As we will see, the Nordic countries consistently rank high on numerous other indicators of a well-functioning society, from homicide rates and economic equality to environmental protection and democracy. This does not mean that the Nordic peoples are inherently better or wiser than other people. It largely reflects the fact that they have had the good fortune to grow up under a combination of circumstances, including prosperity and high life expectancy, that produce a relatively strong sense of existential security. And one of the enduring realities of human behavior seems to be that secure people tend to behave better than desperate ones.

The U.S. ranks 16th on the UN Human Development rankings, which is a respectable rank among 189 countries, but it is by no means the world leader (which in this case is Norway). The U.S. doesn't rank at the top on any of the index's components. It no longer has the world's highest per capita income, ranking 5th among the countries on this table. (Liechtenstein, a tax haven with 38,000 people, ranks first.) The U.S. ranks 14th among these countries in years of expected schooling, and 20th in life expectancy—paying a price for its lack of universal health coverage.

What are the cultural consequences of these conditions?

As we have noted, religion tends to be less important in the lives of secure people than of insecure ones, but a country's historical heritage also plays an important role. Thus, as the top part of Table 8.4 indicates, in each country's latest available Values Survey, fully half of the people of the Nordic countries say they do not believe in God. This figure is much higher than in the past and much higher than in most other countries, but nonbelief in God is exceeded (at 53 percent) by the publics of the Confucian-influenced countries, who grew up in societies that have been relatively secular for centuries. Currently, 31 percent of the publics of the non-Nordic high-income societies say that they do not believe in God, in contrast with only 12 percent of the publics of middle-income and low-income countries and an almost nonexistent share (2 percent) of the population of Muslim-majority countries.

Table 8.4. The declining role of religion

1. Believe in God	
	% No
Nordic countries	50
High-income countries	31
Confucian-influenced countries	53
Middle- and low-income countries	12
Muslim-majority countries	2
2. Believe in an Afterlife	
	% No
Nordic countries	56
High-income countries	48
Confucian-influenced countries	77
Middle- and low-income countries	40
Muslim-majority countries	15
3. Confidence in Churches/Religious Institutions	
	% A Great Deal
Nordic countries	8
High-income countries	10
Confucian-influenced countries	8
Middle- and low-income countries	35
Muslim-majority countries	48

Source: Data from countries included in Waves 6 or 7 of the Values Surveys. These countries are **Nordic**: Denmark, Finland, Iceland, Netherlands, Norway, Sweden; other **High-income**: Andorra, Australia, Austria, France, Germany, Greece, Italy, New Zealand, Spain, Switzerland, United Kingdom, United States; **Confucian-influenced**: China, Hong Kong, Taiwan, Japan, South Korea, Singapore; **Middle- and low-income**: Albania, Argentina, Armenia, Bolivia, Brazil, Bulgaria, Chile, Colombia, Croatia, Cyprus, Czech Republic, Ecuador, Estonia, Georgia, Ghana, Hungary, India, Lithuania, Mexico, Nigeria, Peru, Philippines, Poland, Puerto Rico, Romania, Russia, Rwanda, Slovakia, Slovenia, South Africa, Thailand, Trinidad, Ukraine, Uruguay, Zimbabwe; **Muslim-majority**: Algeria, Azerbaijan, Bangladesh, Indonesia, Iraq, Jordan, Kazakhstan, Kyrgyzstan, Lebanon, Libya, Malaysia, Morocco, Pakistan, Qatar, Tunisia, Turkey, Uzbekistan.

Belief in an afterlife shows a similar pattern (see the next part of Table 8.4): nonbelief in an afterlife has risen to 56 percent in the Nordic countries but is even higher (at 77 percent) in the Confucian-influenced countries, followed by 48 percent in the non-Nordic high-income countries, 40 percent in the middle- and low-income countries, and 15 percent in the Muslim-majority countries. We find the converse pattern concerning confidence in the religious institutions of one's country: the proportion expressing "a great deal of confidence" has fallen to only 8 percent in the Nordic countries and 10 percent in the other high-income countries, and is 8 percent in Confucian-influenced countries—but it is 35 percent among the publics of middle-income and low-income countries and 48 percent in the Muslim-majority countries.

One of the most profound consequences of the shift from religiosity to individual-choice norms is the declining role of the family. As the top section of Table 8.5 indicates, in Muslim-majority countries fully 71 percent of the public strongly agrees with the statement "One of the main goals in my life has been to make my parents proud." This figure drops to 46 percent of the public in middle- and low-income countries, to 23 percent in most high-income countries, and to only 9 percent in the Nordic countries.

The next sections of Table 8.5 tell a similar story. In all but the high-income countries, overwhelming majorities of the population agree that it is a child's duty to take care of an ill parent; however, in most high-income countries the figure is 48 percent, and in the Nordic countries it is only 24 percent. In traditional societies there was little alternative to having family members care for the old, but in modern societies with comprehensive safety nets, it is less necessary. Finally, in Confucian-influenced countries, Muslim-majority countries, and other middle- and low-income societies, majorities or near-majorities agree that it is one's duty to have children. In high-income countries only 24 percent agree, and in the Nordic countries only 11 percent do so. These high-income countries have sufficiently low infant mortality rates and high life expectancy that the pressure to have children is low. The traditional functions of the family in educating the young, providing child care, and taking care of the elderly are giving way to specialized institutions that may do a good job objectively—but the family may have performed these functions in a warmer, more personal way. Modernization brings losses as well as gains. On the other hand, deference to one's elders can discourage openness to new ideas and accepting other kinds of people.

Though less family-oriented than other nationalities, the Nordic peoples are markedly more open to outsiders, as Table 8.6 demonstrates. The Values Surveys offer respondents a list of various types of people, asking, "Could you please mention any that you would not like to have as neighbors?" The people of the Nordic countries are generally less exclusive than others, but

Table 8.5. The declining role of the family

1. One of the main goals in my life has been to make my parents proud.	
	% Agree Strongly
Nordic countries	9
High-income countries	23
Confucian-influenced countries	19
Middle- and low-income countries	46
Muslim-majority countries	71

2. It is the child's duty to take care of an ill parent.	
	% Agree or Strongly Agree
Nordic countries	24
High-income countries	48
Confucian-influenced countries	73
Middle- and low-income countries	78
Muslim-majority countries	87

3. It is one's duty to society to have children.	
	% Agree or Strongly Agree
Nordic countries	11
High-income countries	21
Confucian-influenced countries	59
Middle- and low-income countries	47
Muslim-majority countries	71

Source: Data from countries included in Waves 6 or 7 of the Values Surveys.

this tendency is particularly striking when it comes to accepting people of another religion (see the top part of the table). Only 4 percent of Nordic people mention that they would not like to have people of another religion as neighbors, compared with as much as 31 percent of the population in other countries. The same is true of immigrants and foreign workers: only 9 percent of the people of the Nordic countries say that they would not like to have immigrants or foreign workers as neighbors, compared with as much as 34 percent of the publics of other countries.

Similarly, the Nordic publics are considerably less likely to agree that, when jobs are scarce, employers should give priority to people of their own

Table 8.6. Acceptance of outsiders

1. I would not like to have people of a different religion as neighbors.	
	% Mentioned
Nordic countries	4
High-income countries	6
Confucian-influenced countries	19
Middle- and low-income countries	17
Muslim-majority countries	31

2. I would not like to have immigrants/foreign workers as neighbors.	
	% Mentioned
Nordic countries	9
High-income countries	11
Confucian-influenced countries	26
Middle- and low-income countries	22
Muslim-majority countries	34

3. When jobs are scarce, employers should give priority to (my nationality) over immigrants.	
	% Agree
Nordic countries	32
High-income countries	47
Confucian-influenced countries	72
Middle- and low-income countries	73
Muslim-majority countries	80

Source: Data from countries included in Waves 6 or 7 of the Values Surveys.

nationality over immigrants; only 32 percent of the Nordics take this position, compared with 47 percent of the public in other high-income countries, 72 percent in Confucian-influenced countries, 73 percent in middle- and low-income countries, and 80 percent in Muslim-majority countries.

Overall, the Nordic peoples have an openness to outsiders that is well adapted to an increasingly globalized world.

Relative openness to foreigners is not just a matter of lip service. As Table 8.7 indicates, the Nordic countries spend a higher percentage of their country's gross domestic income on foreign aid than most other countries. Four of the five highest-ranking countries on this table are Nordic countries,

Table 8.7. Percentage of country's GDI spent on foreign aid

Sweden	1.36
Qatar	1.17
Norway	1.14
Denmark	**0.90**
Netherlands	**0.76**
Switzerland	0.68
United Kingdom	0.67
United Arab Emirates	0.68
Finland	**0.55**
Germany	0.49
Belgium	0.40
France	0.36
China	0.36
Austria	0.31
Australia	0.26
Canada	0.25
Ireland	0.22
Iceland	**0.22**
Japan	0.21
Italy	0.21
New Zealand	0.20
Turkey	0.17
United States	0.15
Portugal	0.15
Croatia	0.14
Greece	0.10
Spain	0.12
Slovenia	0.12
Estonia	0.11
Czech Republic	0.10
Slovakia	0.10
Hungary	0.10
Malta	0.10
South Korea	0.09
Poland	0.09
Lithuania	0.08
India	0.076
Latvia	0.07
Israel	0.06
Russia	0.03

Source: OECD, 2017.

with Sweden, Norway, Denmark, and the Netherlands devoting relatively large shares of their gross domestic income (GDI) to foreign aid. Though the United States is the world's largest donor in absolute terms, this reflects the fact that it has a much larger economy than most other countries. On a per capita basis, it ranks 23rd.

The Nordic countries also rank high in terms of economic equality. As seen in Table 8.8, the Nordic countries make up 6 of the 10 countries with the world's lowest Gini indices of economic inequality. The Gini index measures the degree of inequality in the distribution of a country's family income: if income were distributed with perfect equality, the index would be zero; if it were distributed with perfect inequality, the index would be 100. Nordics constitute a majority of the 10 most egalitarian countries—and, apart from Australia, all 10 of these countries are members of the Protestant Europe cultural zone.[3]

Table 8.9 shows the 2017 homicide rates in the 20 countries that rank highest on the UN Development rankings, together with the 10 countries having the highest homicide rates. All six Nordic countries rank among the 16 countries with the lowest murder rates. Liechtenstein ranks first, with 38,000 people and no homicides (although just one murder would give Liechtenstein a higher murder rate than any Nordic country). Two Confucian-influenced countries, Japan and Singapore, also rank among the four countries with the lowest homicide rates, and the six English-speaking countries also do relatively well. The six Nordic countries have relatively low homicide rates, with a median of about 1 per 100,000 people. The U.S. rate is about five times as high as this, and the median homicide rate among the 10 lowest-ranking countries is about 30 times as high.

The Nordic countries lead the world in support for gender equality, as Table 8.10 demonstrates. Even in comparison with other high-income countries, the Nordic publics are about half as likely to say that men have more right to a job than women, and about half as likely to say that men make better political leaders than women. And in comparison with the publics of Muslim-majority countries, the Nordic publics are one-sixteenth as likely to say that men have more right to a job, and about one-eighth as likely to say that men make better political leaders than women,

Again, this is not just a matter of lip service. Women actually hold a relatively large proportion of the authority positions in the Nordic countries. As Table 8.11 indicates, the Nordic countries occupy all six of the highest ranks on the UN Gender Empowerment measure, which is based on the

Table 8.8. Gini indices of economic inequality
(in top 20 countries on UN Development rankings and
countries with highest homicide rates)

Sweden	24.9
Belgium	25.9
Norway	26.8
Germany	27.0
Finland	27.2
Iceland	28.0
Denmark	29.0
Switzerland	29.5
Australia	30.3
Netherlands	30.3
Austria	30.5
Ireland	31.3
Canada	32.1
United Kingdom	32.4
Jamaica	35.0
El Salvador	36.0
New Zealand	36.2
Japan	37.9
Central African Republic	43.6
United States	45.0
Singapore	45.9
Honduras	47.1
Mexico	48.2
Brazil	49.0
Colombia	51.1
Guatemala	53.0
Hong Kong	53.9
South Africa	62.6

Gini indices not available for Liechtenstein, Puerto Rico, or Trinidad.
China's index is 46.5.

The median date of these Gini indices is 2014.

Source: CIA, 2019.

Table 8.9. Homicide rates per 100,000 population in 2017 (in top 20 countries on the UN Development rankings, plus the 10 countries with the highest homicide rates)

Liechtenstein	0.00
Japan	0.28
Iceland	**0.30**
Singapore	0.32
Norway	**0.51**
Switzerland	0.54
Netherlands	**0.55**
Austria	0.66
Ireland	0.80
Australia	0.94
Denmark	**0.98**
New Zealand	0.99
Sweden	**1.08**
Germany	1.18
United Kingdom	1.20
Finland	**1.42**
Canada	1.68
Belgium	1.95
United States	5.35

(Hong Kong data not available)

Mexico	19.26
Central African Republic	19.76
Colombia	25.50
Guatemala	27.26
Brazil	29.53
Trinidad	30.81
South Africa	33.97
Jamaica	47.01
Honduras	56.52
El Salvador	82.84

Source: United Nations, 2019.

Table 8.10. Support for gender equality

1. When jobs are scarce, men should have more right to a job than women.	
	% Agree or Strongly Agree
Nordic countries	4
High-income countries	11
Confucian-influenced countries	38
Middle- and low-income countries	34
Muslim-majority countries	66
2. Men make better political leaders than women do.	
	% Agree or Strongly Agree
Nordic countries	9
High-income countries	16
Confucian-influenced countries	45
Middle- and low-income countries	45
Muslim-majority countries	70

Source: Data from countries included in Waves 6 or 7 of the Values Surveys.

percentage of seats held by women in national parliaments, the percentage of women in economic decision-making positions, and the earned income ratio of males to females.[4]

How well do the people of various countries perform academically? The Program for International Student Assessment (PISA) is a worldwide study carried out by the Organization for Economic Cooperation and Development (OECD), designed to evaluate educational systems by measuring 15-year-old students' scholastic performance on mathematics, science, and reading. It was first performed in 2000 and was then repeated every three years. The average country scores from the 2018 data collection are shown on Table 8.12.

In their average scores on mathematics, science, and reading, the Confucian-influenced countries dominate the world rankings, occupying all of the top four positions and seven of the top nine positions. But even here, the Nordic countries do relatively well. Though the top nine rankings on the PISA scores are dominated by Confucian-influenced publics, Nordic countries occupy four of the next nine positions. And, for now at least, the Nordics have a broader range of strengths than the Confucian-influenced

Table 8.11. Rank on UN gender empowerment measure

---

1 Norway
2 Sweden
3 Finland
4 Denmark
5 Iceland
6 Netherlands
7 Belgium
8 Australia
9 Germany
10 Canada
11 New Zealand
12 Spain
13 Austria
14 United Kingdom
15 United States
16 Singapore
17 Argentina
18 France
19 Ireland
20 Bahamas

81 Bangladesh
82 Pakistan
83 Cambodia
84 Qatar
85 Sri Lanka
86 Nepal
87 Iran
88 Morocco
89 Kyrgyzstan
90 Turkey
91 Egypt
92 Saudi Arabia
93 Yemen

Source: United Nations Development Program, 2009, p. 333.

Table 8.12. Average score on mathematics, science, and reading, PISA 2018

1	China (4 cities)*	579
2	Singapore	556
3	Macao	542
4	Hong Kong	531
5	Estonia	525
6	Japan	520
7	South Korea	520
8	Canada	517
9	Taiwan	517
10	**Finland**	**516**
11	Poland	513
12	Ireland	504
13	Slovenia	503
14	United Kingdom	503
15	New Zealand	502
16	**Netherlands**	**502**
17	**Sweden**	**502**
18	**Denmark**	**501**
19	Germany	500
20	Belgium	500
21	Australia	499
22	Switzerland	498
23	**Norway**	**497**
24	Czech Republic	495
25	United States	495
26	France	494
27	Portugal	492
28	Austria	491
29	Latvia	487
30	Russia	481
31	**Iceland**	**481**
32	Lithuania	479
33	Hungary	479
34	Italy	477
35	Luxembourg	477
36	Belarus	472
37	Croatia	472

Continued

Table 8.12. *Continued*

38	Slovakia	469
39	Israel	465
40	Turkey	463
41	Ukraine	463
42	Malta	459
43	Greece	453
44	Serbia	442
45	Cyprus	438
46	Chile	438
47	United Arab Emirates	434
48	Malaysia	431
49	Romania	428
50	Bulgaria	427
51	Moldova	424
52	Uruguay	424
53	Brunei	423
54	Montenegro	422
55	Albania	420
56	Jordan	416
57	Mexico	416
58	Costa Rica	415
59	Qatar	413
60	Thailand	413
61	Colombia	405
62	Kazakhstan	402
58	Azerbaijan	402
64	Bosnia	402
65	Peru	401
66	Brazil	400
67	North Macedonia	400
68	Argentina	395
69	Georgia	387
70	Saudi Arabia	386
71	Indonesia	382
72	Lebanon	377
73	Morocco	368
74	Panama	365
75	Kosovo	361
76	Philippines	350
77	Dominican Republic	334

*Beijing, Shanghai, Jiangsu, Zhejiang

Source: FactsMaps, 2018.

countries, which currently do extremely well in some areas but perform poorly in others.

Nordicization or Sinification of the World?

At this point, let's discuss a leading alternative to the Nordic countries as role models for the future: the Confucian-influenced countries. These countries have a unique historical heritage. For centuries, it was possible to achieve positions of power, prestige, and prosperity by rising in Confucian bureaucracies through diligent study and passing written examinations. No other culture placed as much emphasis on education, and it has left an enduring imprint. Students with a Confucian cultural heritage have attained outstanding academic achievements not only in East Asia but also in Southeast Asia, Europe, and North America. The role of education has become so crucial to both economic and technological development that it raises the question of whether China is becoming the world's most influential role model. In view of the impressive performances of the Confucian-influenced countries in economic growth and life expectancy, it's an open question. Indeed, for low-income countries, China may seem the most attractive model, having recently risen from being an impoverished and technologically backward country to being rich and powerful. Democracy and environmental protection may be desirable, but for these countries the most pressing goal is to escape poverty.

During the past 40 years, China has shown remarkable economic growth and made impressive progress in education, scientific research, and advanced technology. Since the pragmatists took over in 1978, China has shown exceptionally high economic growth, overtaking the U.S. to become the world's largest manufacturing economy; China now leads the world in the production of solar energy panels, and fully two-thirds of the world's investment in artificial intelligence is being made in China (Economy, 2018).

In response to the COVID-19 pandemic, after a brief period of denial China's leadership responded swiftly and effectively, while the top level of the U.S. government spent months in denial, so that by the spring of 2020, the U.S. had more cases of infection and more pandemic-related deaths than any other country in the world. As one observer noted:

The American president denied the threat, rejected scientific expertise, spread misinformation, and left state and local governments to fend for themselves. . . . With shambolic self-governance, the U.S. government has placed its own citizens in unnecessary peril, while sidelining itself from acting as a global crisis leader in a way that is unprecedented in the last seven decades. China is all too happy to fill the vacuum. (Rapp-Hooper, 2020)

But China's recent success was not inevitable. It was badly governed for most of the past three centuries. And its success did not happen because authoritarian governments are more effective than democracies; in fact, authoritarian governments from Zimbabwe to Venezuela have been textbook examples of mismanagement. China's recent success reflects the adoption of a distinctive version of authoritarian rule developed by Deng Xiaoping that incorporated some of democracy's advantages but is now being abandoned.

In 1978 the Chinese Communist Party's pragmatist faction, led by Deng, set China on a radically different path from the one the communists had followed since taking power. Mao Zedong was a brilliant political innovator who developed ways to arouse intense ideological fervor among illiterate peasants, mobilizing a peasant-based movement that triumphed against seemingly overwhelming odds with a communist victory in 1949. As the leader of the victorious Communist Revolution, Mao took on an almost god-like status.

Unfortunately, what works in winning a civil war is not equally effective in building an industrial society. You can train someone how to shoot a rifle in one day, but it takes years to train a competent metallurgist or agronomist. Mao refused to recognize that long-term success requires experts as well as Reds. Under Mao, China's policies were determined not by the rule of law but by whatever Mao chose to do at a given time, resulting in wild policy swings that could have disastrous consequences. Convinced that he could industrialize China very rapidly by mobilizing mass ideological fervor, Mao ignored expert advice and launched the Great Leap Forward in 1958, building backyard steel mills and modernizing agriculture. But the steel was unusable and grain production collapsed, causing 30 to 50 million deaths by starvation. Mao's position in the Chinese Communist Party (CCP) was eclipsed by the disaster, but his prestige was so great that he was never openly denounced. The Party's direction was taken over by the pragmatic faction's leaders, Liu Shaoqi and Deng Xiaoping, who had warned against the dangers of the Great Leap Forward.

After a self-imposed exile in Shanghai, Mao launched the Great Cultural Revolution in 1966 as a way to regain control of the CCP—ostensibly by purging it of corrupt officials. Once again, he did this by arousing mass ideological fervor, this time mobilizing students against the Party itself. The universities were closed and young Red Guards raided government buildings, parading CCP officials through the streets in dunce caps. Top officials, including Liu and Deng, were publicly criticized, beaten, killed, or sent to do manual labor in the countryside. Since the Communist Party was the only organization except the army that was allowed to organize at the national level, when the Party was driven from office, China fell into chaos. The country was approaching civil war when Mao himself ordered the People's Liberation Army to restore order, but China remained on the brink of chaos until his death in 1976. Almost immediately afterward, the Cultural Revolution's remaining leaders were arrested.

What China has accomplished since then is truly impressive. But it doesn't reflect the superiority of authoritarian rule. Most authoritarian regimes (including China for most of the past 300 years) have been far less impressive. China's recent economic miracle largely reflects Deng's policies of pragmatic market-oriented reforms and a regionally decentralized authoritarian system that made local experimentation possible and transformed the economy from a rigid ideologically driven system to a pragmatic one in which Deng and his colleagues experimented to see what worked (Xu, 2011). They relaxed the tight state control over China's economic and political system that had existed since the 1950s, moving from a state-run economy toward a market-driven economy. This led to annual growth rates of close to 10 percent for more than two decades, rescuing hundreds of millions of Chinese from subsistence-level poverty.

China's success also reflects the fact that the country was governed by competent leaders who attained top office through a system of merit recruitment for limited terms, which was also developed by Deng. He instituted collective leadership that replaced the concentration of power in the hands of one man and established a system under which top officials held office for limited terms. This led to China's being ruled by highly competent people handpicked by Deng, who were peacefully rotated out of office on a predictable schedule, to be replaced by a new cohort of officials who had also been selected on grounds of competence.

In order to establish term limits, Deng instituted mandatory retirement at age 70. He then installed a carefully chosen group of 60-year-olds in the top offices, who ran China for two five-year terms but then faced mandatory retirement. He had placed below them a carefully selected group of 50-year-olds in key positions, so that when the first cohort completed their 10 years in office, they were replaced by the next cohort, who would hold power for the next 10 years. As a result, long after Deng's death in 1997, China was governed by competent people who had been handpicked by Deng and who respected the norms he had established limiting their power. And for more than three decades, the country was run by a system in which decision-making authority was shared among the Party's top officials.

In 2012 a new set of leaders took office, led by Xi Jinping. Since taking office, Xi has skillfully centralized authority under his personal leadership, bringing increased state penetration of society and tighter controls over ideas, culture, and capital. Abandoning the collective rule of his immediate predecessors, Xi assumed leadership of the most important policy committees. He has demanded pledges of personal loyalty from military and Party leaders, eliminating political rivals through sweeping anticorruption campaigns and replacing collective leadership with one-man rule. In 2017, the government opened the way for Xi to serve as president for life by eliminating the constitutional provision limiting the president to two terms. Confirming his intention to remain in office indefinitely, Xi has broken with precedent by not appointing a successor-in-training.

Xi is also reversing Deng's policy of giving increasing leeway to market forces, with the CCP playing an increasingly dominant role in the economy and society. In doing so, he is sacrificing economic effectiveness for central control by the CCP—and himself. New technology is being used to monitor the internet and block access to forbidden content, with roughly two million officials monitoring internet communication. Xi's concentration of power is approaching that of Mao, and "Xi Jinping thought" has been written into the constitution.

Rule by a dictator for life is not a formula for effective governance. A long-standing principle of politics is that absolute power corrupts absolutely. Ruling for decades, Mao became increasingly rigid and held absolute power until the day he died. If Xi becomes dictator for life, China is unlikely to function as well as it has during the past 40 years because rule by that formula has severe inherent disadvantages. Dictators tend to become increasingly rigid as they age and eventually become senile. Even more important, the criterion for elite recruitment shifts from personal competence to unquestioning loyalty to the ruler.

Democracy has spread because it is a relatively good way to govern modern societies, and one of its key advantages is the fact that it's based on merit recruitment for limited terms. The fact that Deng was able to adapt this component of democracy to the Chinese setting played a key role in China's recent success; his economic reforms were implemented by competent leaders and his insistence on collective rule even attained a modest degree of separation of powers, offsetting one-man rule. China's performance since the 1980s unquestionably has been impressive—but a return to the Maoist model is likely to reduce the possibility of China's becoming the world's role model.

Environmental Protection

As we have seen, the publics of Confucian-influenced countries are the top scorers on cross-nationally administered tests of academic achievement. This is an impressive achievement in a world increasingly shaped by knowledge economies. But the Nordic countries are their closest contenders in academic achievement, and they currently have a broader range of strengths than the Confucian-influenced countries.

Environmental protection is one such area. The Environmental Performance Index ranks 180 countries on 24 performance indicators across 10 issue categories covering environmental health and ecosystem vitality. These indicators provide a gauge of how close countries are to established environmental policy goals. The Environmental Performance Index is produced jointly by Yale University and Columbia University in collaboration with the World Economic Forum.

As Table 8.13 demonstrates, all six of the Nordic countries rank among the top 18 (out of 180 countries) on the Environmental Performance Index. Both Japan and Taiwan also do well on this index, though all six Nordic countries outrank them. But China—by far the largest Confucian-influenced country—ranks 120th on the list, having some of the most polluted and unhealthy cities in the world. The Chinese government is striving to improve this situation, and quite probably will do so, but for the time being China is not a particularly attractive place in terms of its environment.

Corruption and Commitment to Democracy

Clean government is another area in which the Nordics perform better than most countries. Transparency International is a Berlin-based organization

Table 8.13. Rankings on Environmental
Protection Index

1	Switzerland
2	France
3	**Denmark**
4	Malta
5	Sweden
6	United Kingdom
7	Luxembourg
8	Austria
9	Ireland
10	Finland
11	Iceland
12	Spain
13	Germany
14	Norway
15	Belgium
16	Italy
17	New Zealand
18	Netherlands
19	Israel
20	Japan
21	Australia
22	Greece
23	Taiwan
24	Cyprus
25	Canada
26	Portugal
27	United States
52	Russia
120	China
160	Liberia
161	Cameroon
162	Swaziland
163	Djibouti
164	Papua New Guinea
165	Eritrea

Table 8.13. *Continued*

166	Mauritania
167	Benin
168	Afghanistan
169	Pakistan
170	Angola
171	Central African Republic
172	Niger
173	Lesotho
174	Haiti
175	Madagascar
176	Nepal
177	India
178	Democratic Republic of Congo
179	Bangladesh
180	Burundi

Source: Wendling et al., 2018.

that has more than 100 chapters worldwide and is dedicated to monitoring corruption. This organization prepares an annual index that ranks 180 countries and territories on their perceived levels of public sector corruption, as rated by experts and business people. It uses a scale of 0 to 100, where 0 indicates very corrupt and 100 indicates very clean.

As seen in Table 8.14, the Nordic countries occupy 6 of the 11 highest rankings, having relatively corruption-free government. Four of the English-speaking countries (Australia, Canada, the United Kingdom, and Ireland) also occupy high rankings, and the United States is not far behind. A Confucian-influenced country, Japan, also holds a high position, but China ranked 80th on the 2019 rankings, almost halfway down the list.

The Nordic publics also have a relatively strong commitment to democracy. Since the collapse of communism, a majority of virtually every public in the world says that democracy is a good thing, but many of them also accept rule by the army or rule by experts or by strong authoritarian leaders. Consequently, the percentage of the public that *rejects* nondemocratic forms of government provides a more realistic measure of popular support for democracy than the percentage who say they favor democracy.

Table 8.14. Transparency International
corruption rankings

---

1 Denmark

1 New Zealand

3 Finland

4 Singapore

4 Sweden

4 Switzerland

7 Norway

8 Netherlands

9 Germany

9 Luxembourg

11 Iceland

12 Australia

12 Austria

12 Canada

12 United Kingdom

16 Hong Kong

17 Belgium

18 Estonia

18 Ireland

20 Japan

23 United States

80 China

80 India

168 Democratic Republic of Congo

168 Guinea Bissau

168 Haiti

168 Libya

172 North Korea

173 Afghanistan

173 Equatorial Guinea

173 Sudan

173 Venezuela

177 Yemen

178 Syria

179 South Sudan

180 Somalia

Source: Transparency International, 2019.

Table 8.15. Support for democracy

1. Political system: Having a strong leader who does not need to bother with the laws or parliament	
	Very Good or Fairly Good
Nordic countries	22
High-income countries	27
Confucian-influenced countries	47
Middle- and low-income countries	52
Muslim-majority countries	52

2. Political action: Signing a petition	
	% Would Never Do
Nordic countries	10
High-income countries	14
Confucian-influenced countries	40
Middle- and low-income countries	51
Muslim-majority countries	69

Source: Data from countries included in Waves 6 or 7 of the Values Surveys.

As Table 8.15 indicates, the publics of the Nordic countries are somewhat less likely to support rule by a strong leader than are the publics of the other high-income countries, and less than half as likely to support "having a strong leader who does not need to bother with the laws or parliament" as are the publics of the Confucian countries, the middle- or low-income countries, or the Muslim-majority countries.

Democracy is most likely to survive if its people actively support it, and the Nordic publics seem likelier to actively participate in politics than the publics of other countries. Here again, we use a negative indicator, showing the percentage saying they would *never* sign a petition. The Nordics are somewhat less likely to say they would never sign a petition than the publics of other high-income countries. But the publics of the Confucian countries are four times as likely to say they never would sign a petition as are the Nordic publics, while the publics of the middle- and low-income countries are five times as likely, and the publics of Muslim-majority countries are almost seven times as likely.

Once again, this is not just a matter of lip service. The oldest and one of the most widely accepted programs for rating democracy is carried out by Freedom House. Since 1972, this nonprofit organization based in New York has used expert ratings to evaluate the state of freedom in countries around the world. Each country is assigned between 0 and 4 points on a series of 25 indicators, including (1) elections to executive, (2) elections to legislature, (3) full political rights for minorities, and (4) freedom from pervasive corruption. These scores are used to determine numerical ratings on two dimensions, political rights and civil liberties, each of which receives ratings that range from 1 (representing the most free conditions) to 7 (the least free). The *Freedom in the World* reports assess the real-world rights and freedoms enjoyed by individuals rather than governments or government performance per se.[5]

Table 8.16 shows Freedom House's 2018 democracy rankings for the 20 highest-ranked countries, plus the U.S. and 10 other countries, based on their combined political rights and civil liberties ratings. Nordic countries get four of the five highest rankings, and Finland, Norway, and Sweden are rated as the world's three most democratic countries. Among Confucian-influenced countries, Japan has the 12th highest rank, but China ranks 145th out of 159 countries with populations over one million.

In 2006, the United States was classified as a "full democracy" and ranked as the world's 17th most democratic country. By 2018 it had declined to 34th place and was rated as a "flawed democracy," having experienced a series of setbacks in the conduct of elections and criminal justice over the previous decade. Moreover, its core institutions were being attacked by a president who had threatened the media for challenging routinely false statements, spoken disdainfully of judges who blocked his decisions, and attacked the professional staff of law enforcement and intelligence agencies.

Because democracy is a hotly contested topic, we also provide rankings from a newer but also highly respected source, the Varieties of Democracy Institute at the University of Gothenburg (the V-Dem Institute). This organization uses innovative methods for aggregating expert judgments in order to produce valid and reliable estimates of difficult-to-observe concepts. This aspect is critical because many key features of democracy are not directly observable and expert-coded data raises concerns about comparability across time and space. The V-Dem Institute has recruited over 3,000 country experts from almost every country of the world to provide their judgments. The Institute typically gathers data from five experts for each observation,

Table 8.16. Freedom House democracy rankings in 2018, based on combined political rights and civil liberties scores

1	Finland
2	Norway
3	Sweden
4	Canada
5	Netherlands
6	Australia
7	New Zealand
8	Uruguay
9	Denmark
10	Ireland
11	Belgium
12	Japan
13	Portugal
14	Switzerland
15	Chile
16	Cyprus
17	Estonia
18	Germany
19	Iceland
20	Slovenia
34	United States
50	India
72	Indonesia
91	Nigeria
102	Bangladesh
105	Pakistan
115	Turkey
129	Russia
145	China
148	Libya
159	Syria

Source: Freedom House, 2019, p. 16. This page shows only countries with populations of one million or more; Iceland's ranking was interpolated based on the scores from the full dataset.

making it possible to statistically account for uncertainty about estimates and potential expert biases.

V-Dem measures hundreds of attributes of democracy. Five key measures are (1) elected officials; (2) free, fair, and frequent elections; (3) associational autonomy; (4) inclusive citizenship; and (5) freedom of expression. These attributes are used to classify countries as closed autocracies, electoral autocracies, electoral democracies, or liberal democracies.

Table 8.17 lists the top 20 countries plus the U.S. and 10 other countries on V-Dem's Liberal Democracy Index. Nordic countries occupy 5 of the top 11 positions. Despite using different methodologies, the democracy ratings produced by Freedom House and V-Dem converge fairly closely, with Nordic countries occupying the top three positions in both systems. Though there is some divergence on details, Norway, Sweden, Denmark, Finland, and the Netherlands never rank lower than 11th place, and by both rating systems Iceland ranks 18th or 19th out of roughly 200 countries.

Traditional and Modern Routes to Happiness

The Nordic countries rank at or near the top of the world by many standards, but we have not yet examined how well they function on what is arguably the most important criterion of all: the extent to which they contribute to their peoples' happiness. There is no simple answer to this question, because there are both modern and traditional routes to happiness.

Can happiness actually be measured? The answer seems to be yes. Over the past 60 years a number of measures have been developed and carefully validated; among the most widely used are the responses to two questions that are about as straightforward as one can get, and for which a long time series is available:

Taking all things together, would you say you are very happy, fairly happy, not very happy, or not at all happy?

and

All things considered, how satisfied are you with your life as a whole these days?

Table 8.17. National rankings in 2018 on
V-Dem's Liberal Democracy Index

1 **Norway**

2 **Sweden**

3 **Denmark**

4 Estonia

5 Switzerland

6 Costa Rica

7 Australia

8 Portugal

9 **Netherlands**

10 New Zealand

11 **Finland**

12 South Korea

13 United Kingdom

14 Belgium

15 Uruguay

16 Italy

17 Germany

18 **Iceland**

19 France

20 Slovenia

27 United States

63 Indonesia

72 India

78 Nigeria

116 Pakistan

136 Libya

147 Bangladesh

161 Turkey

163 Russia

180 China

201 North Korea

Source: V-Dem Institute, 2019, pp. 11–12.

Responses to the second question are given on a 10-point scale, ranging from "completely dissatisfied" to "completely satisfied."

As one would expect, translating these questions into the many languages used around the world is a challenging task. Over the years, I've often heard such claims as "The language of country X has no equivalent for the word 'happiness.'" On closer inspection, this has always proven to be untrue—for good reason. Some concepts are, indeed, untranslatable, but everyone is aware of whether they are too hot or too cold and whether they are happy or unhappy. This is not true of abstract concepts such as "democracy." People do not have an immediate, firsthand awareness of whether or not they live in a democracy. The concept has widely differing meanings and is further complicated by the fact that today, the governments of most countries—even the most blatantly undemocratic ones—claim to be democratic. As a result, the people of most countries (including China and Vietnam) claim to be living in democracies even when empirical analysis indicates what they have in mind is almost the exact opposite of what is specified by democratic theory (Welzel, 2013).

This is not true of the concepts of happiness and life satisfaction, which show similar attitudinal and societal correlates cross-culturally. In response to most survey questions, anywhere from 3 to 50 percent of the public give no response, either because they don't understand the question or because they've never thought about the topic. In response to the questions about happiness and life satisfaction, nonresponse is virtually nonexistent in countries around the world. People have an immediate awareness of whether their shoes are too tight.

But measuring human happiness is further complicated by another fact: there are both traditional and modern routes to happiness, and they have contrasting relationships with religion. The three following statements seem contradictory, but they are empirically true:

1. Within any country, religious people are generally happier than nonreligious people.
2. Highly religious countries are poorer than nonreligious ones.
3. The people of rich countries are happier and more satisfied with their lives than the people of poor countries.

This reflects the fact that, for centuries, religion helped people cope with life even when facing starvation, disease, and oppression. But developed countries have found ways to reduce or eliminate starvation, disease, oppression, and xenophobia. This is conducive to happiness and life satisfaction—but it reduces the role of religion.

The result is that people of high-income countries tend to be happier than those of low-income countries. This is not surprising, since those in high-income countries have the advantages of prosperity, freedom from hunger, lower crime rates, higher life expectancy, lower infant mortality, air conditioning, and many other things. They also have developed relatively tolerant cultures, which are closely linked with high levels of subjective well-being (R. Inglehart et al., 2008; R. F. Inglehart, 2018, pp. 140–72). Accordingly, the people of high-income countries have relatively high levels of life satisfaction.

But this tendency is weaker than one might expect, because belief systems can compensate for the lack of material advantages. As portrayed in Figure 8.1, high-income countries show low levels of religiosity and high levels of life satisfaction; the Nordic publics show even higher life satisfaction than the publics of the other high-income countries. But despite their relatively low levels on almost all the indicators we have just examined, the publics of

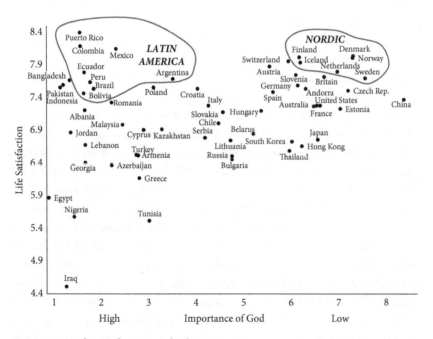

Figure 8.1 Life satisfaction and religiosity.

Source: Based on data from the 2017–9 Values Surveys.

Latin American countries also show relatively high levels of life satisfaction, with Puerto Rico, Colombia, and Mexico showing especially high levels. This is not a fluke. It has been an enduring finding of the Values Surveys for the past 20 years.

At this point in history, Latin Americans have strong religiosity and have adopted democracy, same-sex marriage, gender quotas in parliament, tolerance of ethnic minorities, and other aspects of tolerant, modern cultures. They have attained some of the advantages of modernity while retaining high levels of religiosity that can also contribute to subjective well-being.

Even more surprisingly, the publics of Bangladesh, Pakistan, and Indonesia also rank relatively high on life satisfaction—and, turning to Table 8.2, one finds that these are the three *lowest*-ranking countries on the religiosity/individual-choice index, at the opposite end of the scale from the Nordic countries. These are among the countries that have been *least* involved in the shift from religiosity to individual-choice norms, and they rank even higher on religiosity than most Latin American countries. Perhaps because they embody the traditional worldview most fully, in which religion compensates for the absence of prosperity, freedom, and health, they show life satisfaction levels almost as high as those of the Nordic countries. But this is only a conjecture, for the publics of other strongly religious countries, such as Egypt, Nigeria, and Iraq, show very low levels of life satisfaction; moreover, Bangladesh, Pakistan, and Indonesia did not show particularly high life satisfaction levels in previous surveys.

This is not true of the Latin American countries, which have consistently shown surprisingly high levels of life satisfaction. Figure 8.2 shows the relationship between life satisfaction and per capita GDP in 95 countries containing 90 percent of the world's population.[6] To maximize reliability, this figure is based on the data from all of the Values Surveys carried out from 1981 to 2014. These countries' mean life satisfaction scores are plotted against per capita GDP in 2000. The curve on this figure shows the logarithmic regression line for the relationship between per capita GDP and life satisfaction. If each society's life satisfaction level were wholly determined by its level of economic development, every country would fall on the regression line. Most countries are fairly close to this line, which shows a curve of diminishing returns. At the low end, even small economic gains bring substantial gains in subjective well-being—but the curve levels off among rich countries, and at the high end further economic gains bring little further

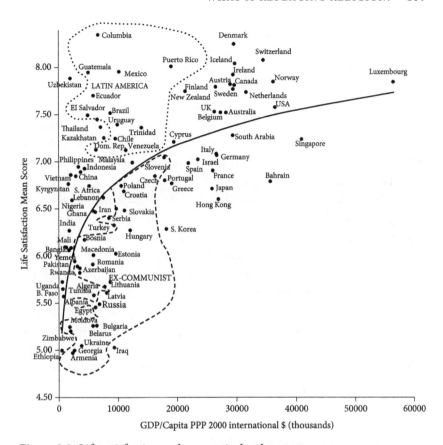

Figure 8.2 Life satisfaction and economic development.

Source: R. F. Inglehart, 2018, p. 151. Based on data from all available WVS/EVS carried out from 1981 through 2014. GDP/capita in purchasing power parity estimates in 2000 from World Bank.

gains in subjective well-being. A country's GDP and its life satisfaction level correlate at r = .60, which suggests that economic development has an important impact on subjective well-being, but that it is only part of the story. For an impoverished country, the most effective way to increase life satisfaction may be to maximize economic growth—but maximizing it in a high-income country requires a different strategy.

The cultural changes linked with modernization can be seen as a shift from maximizing one's chances of survival by striving for economic and physical security to maximizing subjective well-being through cultural and societal changes. This shift in strategies seems to work: people who emphasize self-expression values show higher levels of happiness and life satisfaction than those who emphasize survival values; people who live in democracies show higher levels of happiness than people who live in authoritarian societies.

For desperately poor people, economic gains have a major impact on happiness: at starvation level, happiness can almost be defined as getting enough to eat. As one moves from desperately poor countries like Zimbabwe and Ethiopia to slightly less impoverished countries, the curve rises sharply—but when one reaches the level of Cyprus or Slovenia, the curve levels off. Although Luxemburg is twice as rich as Denmark, the Danes are happier than the Luxembourgers.

The four Latin American countries with the highest happiness ratings on Figure 8.1 (Colombia, Puerto Rico, Mexico, and Ecuador) also show exceptionally high levels of life satisfaction. Is it possible that their high levels are simply an artifact of translation—that "satisfaction" implies a higher level than "satisfaccion"? That doesn't seem to be the case. For one thing, the people of these four countries consistently rank higher than the people of other Spanish-speaking countries—including Spain, which actually ranks *below* the regression line. (And the people of Brazil rank much higher than those of Portugal.) The people of Colombia, Puerto Rico, Mexico, and Ecuador rank much higher on both happiness and life satisfaction than their economic level would predict, and this seems to go deeper than an artifact of translation.

The people of the (linguistically rather diverse) Nordic countries also consistently rank exceptionally high on both life satisfaction and happiness, and the differences are substantial. In Denmark, 52 percent of the public said that they were highly satisfied with their lives (placing themselves at 9 or 10 on a 10-point scale), and 45 percent said they were very happy. In Armenia, only 5 percent were highly satisfied with their lives, and just 6 percent were very happy. In contrast with the modest differences found *within* most countries, the cross-national differences are huge.

As Figure 8.2 shows, Denmark, Iceland, Norway, Sweden, Finland, and the Netherlands all fall well above the regression line, having higher levels of life satisfaction than their per capita GDP would predict, having some of the highest life satisfaction levels in the world. And while Indonesia shows a moderately high life satisfaction level, Bangladesh and Pakistan rank much lower.

Among the remaining countries, we find two distinctive groups: (1) former communist countries and (2) Latin American societies. Although these two groups have roughly similar income levels, the Latin American countries consistently show much higher levels of both life satisfaction and happiness than the ex-communist countries. All 12 of the Latin American countries for which we have data fall above the regression line, showing higher levels of subjective well-being than their economic levels would predict, while almost all of the ex-communist societies show lower levels of subjective well-being than their economic levels would predict; indeed, Russia and several other former Soviet states show lower levels than much poorer countries.

Life satisfaction and happiness produce similar patterns: the Latin American societies are overachievers and the ex-communist societies are underachievers on both indicators of subjective well-being. In the Latin American countries, an average of 45 percent of the population described themselves as very happy, and 42 percent rated themselves as very satisfied with their lives as a whole; in the ex-communist countries, only 12 percent described themselves as very happy, and only 14 percent were very satisfied with their lives.

Communist rule is not necessarily linked with low levels of subjective well-being; China and Vietnam, still ruled by communist parties and enjoying high rates of economic growth, showed much higher levels of well-being than the Soviet successor states. But the collapse of their political, economic, and belief systems seems to have sharply reduced the subjective well-being of the other ex-communist societies.

Regression analyses of the factors conducive to subjective well-being find that high levels of religiosity at Time 1 predict relatively high levels of subjective well-being at a later time (see R. Inglehart et al., 2008). These regression analyses indicate that the extent to which people live in a tolerant society *also* helps shape subjective well-being, even when we control for economic development. Intolerant social norms rigidly restrict people's life choices, reducing subjective well-being. Tolerance of gender equality, gays and lesbians, and people of other religions has a significant impact on subjective well-being. It is not just that being tolerant makes one happy—living in a tolerant social environment seems to be conducive to happiness for everyone.[7]

In Figure 8.3 happiness shows a relationship with religiosity that is similar to the pattern shown in Figure 8.1. Here again, the people of the Nordic countries have some of the highest levels of subjective well-being among all the countries of the world, and their happiness levels are even higher than those of most other high-income countries. The Nordic people's high happiness levels are not caused by their low levels of religiosity, of course. They reflect the fact that cultural change brings changing strategies to maximize human

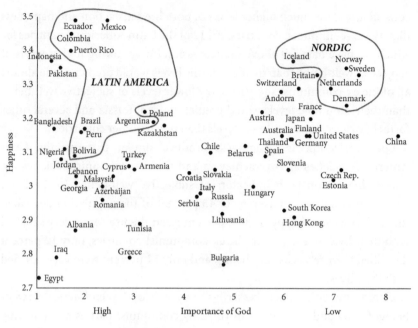

Figure 8.3 Happiness and religiosity.

happiness. In agrarian societies| with little or no economic development or social mobility, religion makes people happier by lowering their aspirations in this life and promising that they will be rewarded in an afterlife. But modernization brings economic development, democratization, and growing social tolerance—which are conducive to happiness because they give people more freedom of choice| in how to live their lives. Consequently, although *within* most countries religious people are happier than less religious people, the people of modernized but secular countries are happier than the people of less modernized but highly religious countries. Thus, though religion is conducive to happiness under premodern conditions, once high levels of economic development become possible, the modern strategy can be even more effective than the traditional strategy as a way to maximize happiness.

The extent to which a society allows free choice has a major impact on happiness, as R. F. Inglehart (2018, pp. 140–72) demonstrates. During the three decades after 1981, economic development, democratization, and rising social tolerance increased the extent to which people in most countries have free choice in economic, political, and social life, resulting in higher levels of happiness. But four Latin American countries consistently show exceptionally high levels of both happiness and life satisfaction. There seem to be two different ways to maximize human happiness and life satisfaction, one linked with religion and another linked with modernization—and for the time being certain Latin American countries enjoy the advantages of both worlds, having high levels of social tolerance while still being relatively religious. Certain Muslim-majority countries also show relatively high levels of subjective well-being, though this is inconsistent over time and space. But, as the evidence presented in this book indicates, the route linked with modernization seems to be spreading pervasively, and the version that has emerged in the Nordic countries may be the wave of the future.

Nordic people are not happy because they're less religious but because their synthesis of advanced social policies and key elements of their Protestant heritage has made their societies relatively secure and egalitarian. They are less dependent on religion than they once were, but they have high levels of interpersonal trust, tolerance, honesty, social solidarity, gender equality, and commitment to democratic norms, all of which are conducive to subjective well-being. And as we have seen, they rank among the world's healthiest, best educated, and most prosperous countries.

The Nordic synthesis is impressive, but it has not gone unchallenged. President Trump, for example, has claimed that countries like Sweden are the real enemy, equating social democracy with totalitarian communism. In a sense, Trump's hostility is logical, for the Nordic model represents the exact opposite of almost everything he stands for. The following chapter examines the forces that threaten to bring this model down.

9

At What Point Does Even Sweden Get a Xenophobic Party?

Economic and physical insecurity encourage xenophobia, authoritarian politics, and rigid adherence to traditional norms. Throughout history human survival was usually insecure, and one successful strategy was to close ranks behind a strong leader, the rise of Hitler being a tragic recent example.

Germany has come a long way from the crimes against humanity that Germans committed during the Nazi era. When West Germany emerged as an independent nation in 1949 it adopted democratic institutions and launched extensive programs to reeducate the German public about the horrors of the Holocaust. The process took time, but by the 1970s a pro-democratic political culture had taken root among a majority of the West German public (R. Inglehart, 1977, pp. 106–8). In subsequent years, strong xenophobic right-wing parties emerged in neighboring countries, but a solid majority of the German public seemed to have become immune to the appeals of any party resembling the Nazis, and no extreme-right party ever drew enough of the national vote to rise above the 5 percent threshold required to enter Parliament. A democratic political culture evolved to the point where, by the 21st century, a reunited Germany ranked higher on democracy than the U.S., according to both Freedom House and the Varieties of Democracy Institute.

In 2015, as desperate Syrian refugees poured into Europe, the German government, led by Angela Merkel, opened the country's borders to all asylum seekers. It was a bold and generous act, and it brought a surge of almost a million new refugees—mainly Muslim—into Germany in one year. But Germany's immunity to xenophobic right-wing parties suddenly ended in the September 2017 national elections, when support for the xenophobic, authoritarian, populist Alternative for Germany party surged from an insignificant level to more than 13 percent of the total vote, making it Germany's

Religion's Sudden Decline. Ronald F. Inglehart, Oxford University Press (2021). © Oxford University Press.
DOI: 10.1093/oso/9780197547045.003.0009

third largest party. The two governing parties, the Christian Democrats and the Social Democrats, scored their worst electoral results of the postwar era, winning 33 percent and 20 percent of the vote, respectively.

To a large extent this change reflected opposition to Merkel's open-door policy for refugees. Surveys showed that 89 percent of the Alternative for Germany voters thought that her immigration policies ignored the concerns of the German people, and 85 percent of them wanted stronger national borders. The governing parties subsequently abandoned immigrant-welcoming policies, and the Alternative for Germany continued to make strong showings in regional elections and in the 2019 elections to the European Parliament.

The sad truth seems to be that no country can absorb an unlimited influx of immigrants without triggering a reaction that can undermine the principles motivating their admission. There is not a fixed numerical threshold; the strength of the reaction is also shaped by the socioeconomic environment. Thus, for example, support for the Alternative for Germany is twice as high in the economically insecure former East German region as it is in the more prosperous former West Germany. The reaction also reflects the rate of change: diversity is not in itself destabilizing, but rapid change is. In already diverse settings, significant inflows of newcomers may not seem threatening because people have grown up with diversity and it seems normal. But in more homogeneous settings, even relatively small absolute numbers of newcomers can trigger cultural anxiety.

The Nordic countries and the Netherlands have even longer traditions of tolerance than those that emerged in Germany after World War II. The Netherlands has been a refuge for people fleeing religious persecution since the 17th century, when Spanish and Portuguese Jews fled the Inquisition, and this continued through World War II, when Dutch families risked their lives to shelter Jews. Similarly, during the German occupation, the Danes managed to smuggle almost all of Denmark's Jews to safety in Sweden. Nevertheless, the grim reality is that today, every Nordic country except Iceland (which has very little immigration) has a strong and influential anti-immigrant party.

How did this happen?

It seems to reflect a deep-rooted emotional response to the threat of invasion, triggered by large-scale immigration in a setting of rapid cultural change and declining economic security.

The Authoritarian Reflex: An Enduring Phenomenon

The concept of the authoritarian personality has been prominent since the 1950s. Though its original theoretical basis and the instrument used to measure it have been superseded, over the past seven decades scores of empirical studies have confirmed that there is a pervasive tendency for deference to authority to be linked with xenophobia, intolerance, and conformity to group norms. But authoritarianism is both a relatively stable personality attribute and a response to the current socioeconomic environment (R. F. Inglehart, 2018, 173–88). It seems to reflect a deep-rooted reaction to insecurity that may have evolved in hunting-and-gathering societies. An updated measure of authoritarianism, the right-wing authoritarianism battery, has become widely used. It taps authoritarianism, conservatism, and traditionalism—three related strategies for attaining collective security (Duckitt & Bizumic, 2013; Duckitt et al., 2010). But authoritarianism also seems to reflect an even broader response to insecurity that has been explored by other investigators under such names as "materialism-postmaterialism," "individualism-collectivism," and "tight-loose cultures" (Chiao & Blizinsky, 2009; Fincher et al., 2008; Gelfand et al., 2011; Hofstede, 2001; R. F. Inglehart, 2018, pp. 12–4, 172–88; Thornhill et al., 2010). This enduring phenomenon continues to be relevant today and helps explain the global surge of support for xenophobic populism that includes Trump, Brexit, and the Alternative for Germany.

Evolutionary modernization theory holds that economic and physical insecurity are conducive to xenophobia, in-group solidarity, authoritarian politics, and rigid adherence to traditional cultural norms—and conversely that secure conditions lead to greater tolerance of outgroups, openness to new ideas, and more egalitarian social norms (R. Inglehart & Welzel, 2005; R. F. Inglehart, 2018). Evolution has shaped all organisms to give top priority to survival; organisms that did not do so died out. Consequently, people evolved to give top priority to obtaining whatever survival needs are in short supply.

Throughout history human survival was usually insecure; the population increased to absorb the food supply and then was held constant by starvation, disease, and violence. Under these conditions, societies tend to emphasize strong in-group solidarity, conformity to group norms, rejection of outsiders, and obedience to strong leaders. For under extreme scarcity, xenophobia is realistic: if there is just enough land to support one tribe and another tribe moves in, survival becomes a zero-sum struggle. One successful strategy is for the tribe to close ranks behind a strong leader, forming a united front against outsiders, a strategy that I call the authoritarian reflex. For authoritarianism is only partly a personality trait; it is also a reaction to current levels of existential insecurity. These two aspects of authoritarianism correspond to cohort effects and period effects, respectively, in birth cohort analysis.

Survey evidence indicates that deference to authority, conformism, and xenophobia increases in times of insecurity (Brader et al., 2008; Gorodzeisky & Semyonov, 2016). Historical evidence too points to this conclusion, the classic example being Germany's Weimar Republic. Under the relatively secure conditions of 1928, most Germans viewed the Nazis as a lunatic fringe party, giving them less than 3 percent of the vote in national elections. But in 1932, after the Great Depression had struck, the Nazis won 44 percent of the vote, becoming the strongest party in the Reichstag and taking over the government soon after. The Great Depression brought widespread unemployment and starvation, and during this era many other countries, from Spain to Japan, also fell under Fascist rule. Though some people are more predisposed to authoritarianism than others, severe existential insecurity triggers an authoritarian reflex that brings higher levels of xenophobia and authoritarian conformity. Thus, though intergenerational population replacement is eroding the demographic base of authoritarianism, the coronavirus pandemic of 2020 could bring a major recession, stimulating the anxieties that fuel the authoritarian reflex.[1]

The coronavirus pandemic provides a natural experiment that makes it possible to test the impact of a threat to survival on people's worldviews by comparing their attitudes before and after it struck. The fact that the pandemic is a life-threatening event was made clear to everyone by the sudden closing of businesses, schools, and public events, generating widespread fear that survival was threatened. Theoretically, this should make people yearn for a strong leader who can lead them to safety. In the U.S., Trump's response to the pandemic veered from months of denial to his claiming to be a wartime president; partly because of this delayed response, by late March 2020 the U.S. had more confirmed coronavirus cases than any other country in the world. At that point—to the surprise of many observers—Trump's approval rating briefly rose to the highest level he had attained since becoming president.

This surge of approval came despite his erratic handling of the crisis, but it was what the authoritarian reflex thesis would predict. The coronavirus pandemic generated even greater surges of support for the leaders of other countries. Over similar time spans, the pandemic approval boost for Italy's chief of government was 27 points; for France's chief of government, the approval boost was 14 points; in Germany the boost was 11 points; and for Trump, the boost was only 5 points and soon subsided.[2] Although insecurity tends to trigger an authoritarian reflex, the response also reflects people's perception of how good a job the leader is doing. Within the U.S., New York had become the pandemic's epicenter, but an overwhelming majority of New Yorkers, 87 percent of eligible voters, thought that Governor Andrew Cuomo was doing a good job: just 11 percent disapproved (Hogan, 2020).

The coronavirus stimulated the anxieties that fuel the authoritarian reflex. Conversely, high levels of existential security are conducive to greater individual autonomy and more openness to diversity and change. Thus, the unprecedentedly high levels of existential security that emerged in high-income countries during the years following World War II brought an intergenerational shift from materialist values emphasizing economic and physical security above all to postmaterialist values emphasizing freedom of expression and openness to outgroups (R. Inglehart, 1971, 1977). These values are the diametric opposite of authoritarianism's xenophobic conformism.

Survey data from countries containing over 90 percent of the world's population indicates that from 1945 to the 1970s, exceptionally high levels of economic and physical security were reshaping human values and motivations in high-income countries, bringing a shift toward more open, tolerant societies. But since then, despite considerable economic growth, the gains have gone almost entirely to the wealthiest, and a growing share of the population has experienced declining real income and job security. In 1970, the largest U.S. employer was General Motors, where workers earned the equivalent of $50 per hour in 2016 dollars. Today, the largest employer, Walmart, pays about $8 per hour in constant dollars. Although the economy as a whole showed substantial growth, men without a bachelor's degree have seen their real wages fall for half a century and their prospects have been dim, contributing to a massive rise in deaths of despair from drug abuse, alcohol abuse, and suicide. Largely due to this, U.S. life expectancy at birth declined for three consecutive years, from 2015 through 2017—something that had not occurred for more than a century (Case & Deaton, 2020, p. 92).

Artificial intelligence has been undermining the economic position of even the more educated, with computer programs taking over the jobs of college-educated workers and those with graduate degrees (R. F. Inglehart, 2018, p. 201). As a noted economist pointed out, "The last 40 years have seen the growth of a semi-permanent upper class that is increasingly isolated from the rest of society" (Milanovic, 2020, p. 14). In the United States, the top 10 percent of the population now own more than 90 percent of the wealth, the remaining 90 percent holding just 10 percent. Soaring inequality, together with rapid cultural change and large-scale immigration, have brought a regression toward xenophobia and authoritarian conformism.

The Backlash against Rapid Cultural Change

The shift from religion to individual-choice norms is playing a major role in the emergence of xenophobic authoritarian movements. As Figure 9.1 demonstrates, in the 2016 U.S. presidential elections, people who scored high on the religiosity end of the religiosity/individual-choice dimension were much likelier to vote for Donald Trump than Hillary

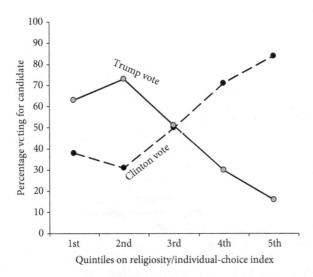

Figure 9.1 Percentage voting for Hillary Clinton and Donald Trump in the 2016 U.S. presidential election, by score on the religiosity/individual-choice norms index.

Source: Data from the U.S. component of the World Values Survey carried out in March–April 2017.

Clinton compared to people who emphasized individual-choice norms. Specifically, among those in the lowest quintile on this dimension, 63 percent voted for Trump and only 37 percent voted for Clinton, but among the highest quintile, 84 percent voted for Clinton and only 16 percent voted for Trump.

Evidence from the Gallup International survey of the 2019 elections to the European Parliament gives additional perspective on the polarization between religiosity and new cultural norms. As Table 9.1 shows, factor analysis of the data from this survey produces a dimension roughly similar to the religiosity/individual-choice dimension—but replacing the individual-choice items with items from the right-wing authoritarianism battery reveals the close linkage between religiosity and authoritarianism. At one pole of this dimension we find people who believe that "homosexuals and feminists should be praised for being brave enough to defy traditional family values" and that "people should pay less attention to the Bible and the other traditional forms of religious guidance" and who rarely or never attend religious services. At

Table 9.1. Religiosity versus new cultural norms* (Principal component analysis)

	Religiosity vs.new norms
Homosexuals and feminists should be praised for being brave enough to defy traditional family values.	.714
People should pay less attention to the Bible and the other old traditional forms of religious guidance, and instead develop their own personal standards of what is moral and immoral.	.543
Apart from weddings or funerals, about how often do you attend religious services? (highest score = never)	.516
Our country will be destroyed some day if we do not smash the perversions eating away at our moral fiber and traditional beliefs.	−.575
The only way our country can get through the crisis ahead is to get back to our traditional values, put tough leaders in power, and silence the troublemakers spreading bad ideas.	−.636
Disapprove of same-sex marriage.	−.780

Source: Data from Gallup International, 2019 European Election Study.
As Figure 9.2 demonstrates, the answer is "A great deal."

In the 2019 European Election study, respondents were asked, "We have a number of parties in [THIS COUNTRY] each of which would like to get your vote. How probable is it that you will ever vote for the following parties? Please answer on a scale where 0 means 'not at all probable' and 10 means 'very probable.'"

the opposite pole we find people who disapprove of same-sex marriage and believe that "the only way our country can get through the crisis ahead is to get back to our traditional values, put tough leaders in power, and silence the troublemakers spreading bad ideas." The factor analysis shown in Table 9.1 generates scores for each respondent. This enables us to answer the question "To what extent does one's position on the Religiosity vs. New Cultural norms dimension shape one's political behavior?"

In the United Kingdom, respondents were asked how probable it was that they might vote for the Conservatives, the Labor Party, the Liberal Democrats, and other parties. including the newly formed Brexit Party organized by Nigel Farage (which took the same xenophobic and anti-European stance as its predecessor, the United Kingdom Independence Party). Despite its newness, this party won 31 percent of the U.K. vote in the European Parliament election. And as Figure 9.2 indicates, the likelihood that a person would support it was strongly influenced by that person's position on the religiosity/new cultural norms dimension. Among those falling into the first (most religious and authoritarian) quintile, the mean score on the 10-point scale was 3.78, which could be interpreted as meaning that the average respondent thought there was about a 38 percent chance that he or

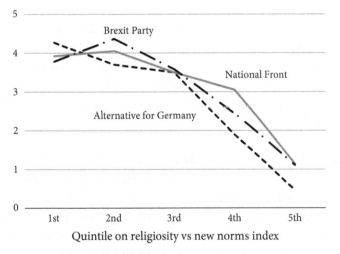

Figure 9.2 Probability of voting for Alternative for Germany, National Rally (former National Front, France), and Brexit Party (U.K.) by quintiles on religiosity/new cultural norms dimension.

Source: Based on data from Gallup International, 2019 European Election Survey.

she might vote for the Brexit Party. But among those in the fifth (least religious and authoritarian) quintile, the mean score fell to 1.11, suggesting a slightly better than 10 percent chance of voting for that party.

The results from France tell a similar story. Among those in the most religious/authoritarian first quintile, the mean estimated probability of voting for the National Rally Party (the newly formed successor to the anti-immigrant National Front) was almost 4 on a 10-point scale. Among those in the fifth quintile, the estimated probability of voting for the National Rally was 1.1, roughly a 1-in-10 chance. The responses of the German public are similar: among the relatively religious and authoritarian first quintile, the mean probability of voting for the Alternative for Germany was 4.27; among the fifth quintile, the mean estimated probability was 0.46, less than one-ninth as high as that of the first quintile.

Table 9.2 analyzes the probability of voting for seven different authoritarian populist parties in their respective countries: the Alternative for Germany, the National Rally, the Brexit Party, the Northern League (Italy), the Austrian Freedom Party, the Law and Justice Party (Poland), and the Hungarian Civic Union (known as Fidesz). The strongest predictors of voting for an authoritarian populist party are the following:

1. The respondent emphasizes religion and authoritarianism rather than the new cultural norms.
2. The respondent feels insecure concerning the economic outlook for the next year.
3. The respondent favors a restrictive immigration policy.

4 and 5. The respondent is older and has fewer years of education.

6. The respondent is willing to restrict individual privacy rights in order to combat crime.

The religiosity/new cultural norms indicator is by far the strongest predictor, and as we have seen, those who score in the first quintile on this dimension are several times as likely to vote for an authoritarian populist party as are those who score in the fifth quintile. As expected, economic insecurity and opposition to immigration are also conducive to voting for these parties, but they are not the proximate drivers. And younger and more educated respondents are less likely to vote for them. But neither income nor social class shows a significant impact on the authoritarian populist vote. A reaction against cultural change, more than economic hardship, drives the authoritarian reflex.

Table 9.2. Predictors of vote for an authoritarian populist party (dependent variable is respondent's score on probability of voting for an authoritarian populist party)

Independent Variables:	Model 1	Model 2	Model 3	Model 4	Model 5	Model 6
Religiosity vs. new norms index	-.327	-.292	-.267	-.271	-.263	-.247
Positive economic outlook for next 12 months	—	-.159	-.149	-.141	-.143	-.131
Oppose restrictive immigration policy	—	—	-.144	-.150	-.147	-.142
Respondent's age	—	—	—	.081	.111	.117
Respondent's education	—	—	—	—	-.109	-.109
Support restricting privacy to combat crime	—	—	—	—	—	.094
Constant	3.91	5.71	6.32	7.00	9.07	8.40
Adjusted R-squared	.11	.13	.15	.16	.17	.18
N =	3,355	3,355	3,355	3,355	3,355	3,355

Cell entry is standardized regression coefficient.

All entries are significant above .000 level.

Source: Data from Gallup International 2019, European Election Study.

Does Declining Religiosity Result
in Corruption and Crime?

One of the societal functions of religion has been to reduce crime and encourage compliance with law. Every major religion teaches some version of "Thou shalt not steal" and "Thou shalt not kill," and historically they seem to have been reasonably effective (Pinker, 2011). Will the decline of religion bring rising crime and corruption? Let's examine the evidence.

Since 1993, Transparency International has been monitoring the extent to which government officials and business people in various countries behave corruptly or honestly publishing an annual Corruption Perception Index that ranks the perceived level of public sector corruption in 180 societies. This makes it possible to test the actual impact of religiosity on corruption: Is corruption less widespread in religious countries than elsewhere? Figure 9.3 shows the relationship between corruption, as measured by a country's score on Transparency International's Corruption Perception Index, and its level

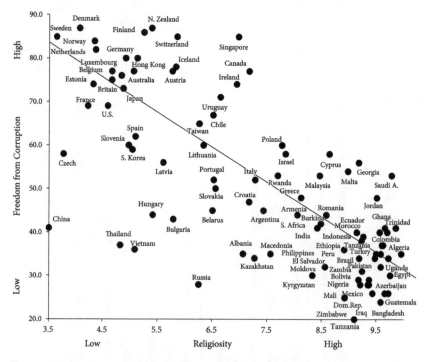

Figure 9.3 Mean score on Transparency International's Corruption Perception Index in 2019, by country's mean level of religiosity (r = −.73).

of religiosity, as measured by its public's response to the question "How important is God in your life?" in its most recent available survey (carried out around 2018).

The results are surprisingly strong and unequivocal: countries with relatively religious publics do *not* show lower levels of corruption than other countries. Quite the contrary, there is a remarkably strong tendency for religious countries to have *higher* levels of corruption than secular countries. High scores on the Transparency International index indicate relatively corruption-free societies, and the overall correlation between religiosity and the corruption index in almost 100 countries is −.73 (statistically significant at the .0001 level). Secular countries are much likelier to have low levels of corruption than religious ones. In the upper-left corner of Figure 9.3 we find the Nordic countries and other stable democracies, which rank low on both religiosity and corruption. In the opposite corner, we find Zimbabwe, Tanzania, Iraq, Bangladesh, and Guatemala, which have highly religious publics and rank among the world's most corrupt countries. To an astonishingly strong degree, religion is linked with corruption, not integrity.

We do not think that religiosity causes corruption. The linkage seems to reflect the fact that countries with low levels of existential security tend to have both high levels of religiosity and high levels of corruption. But it also suggests that, while religion may once have played a crucial role in supporting public morality, that is no longer true.

We should note that the people of religious countries are slightly more likely to *condemn* corruption than the people of less religious countries— but this does not extend to their actual behavior. Religion may make people more punitive, but it does not make them less corrupt.

Let's make another test of the relationship between religiosity and public morality. Are the people of religious countries less likely to commit murder than the people of secular countries? Again, the answer is a resounding no. In fact, as Figure 9.4 demonstrates, the intentional homicide rate per 100,000 people for the 22 countries in the *least* religious quintile of the roughly 100 countries for which we have data is 1.24, while the murder rate for the 22 countries in the *most* religious quintile is 13.03. In short, the murder rate is more than **10 times as high** in the most religious countries as it is in the least religious countries.

Again, we do not think that religiosity causes high murder rates. It seems likelier that the most religious countries have relatively high murder rates because their people are poorer and less secure than those of less religious

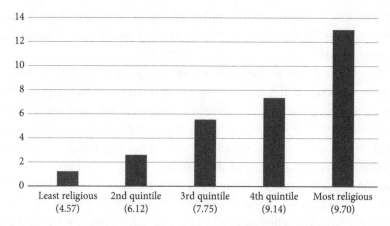

Figure 9.4 Murder rate per 100,000 people, in secular and religious countries. The mean importance of God in one's life for each group of countries (as measured on a 10-point scale in the latest available survey, around 2017) is shown in parentheses below each column. Each quintile contains about 20 countries (listed in Table A.3 of the appendix).

Source: Intentional homicide rates are from UN Office on Drugs and Crime's International Homicide Statistics database, downloaded from Index Mundi, n.d.

countries. But the results also indicate that we do not need to worry that, without religion, people will become murderous and corrupt. In fact, helping them attain reasonably high levels of economic, physical, and social security seems to be an even more effective way of reducing crime than instilling fear of divine punishment.

This may not always have been the case. In the zero-sum economies of agrarian society, people often lived just above survival level, and the option of providing high levels of existential security did not exist. Religion may then have been the most effective available option. Even today, some relatively poor countries, such as Benin, Indonesia, Jordan, and Uzbekistan, have murder rates as low as those of Denmark, Norway, and Sweden. But the overall tendency is for prosperous countries with high levels of existential security to have much lower murder rates than poor countries.

Cultural evolution has been moving in a direction that makes societies progressively less dependent on religion in order to maintain public morality. For, along with the decline of traditional religiosity, an at least equally strong set of moral norms has been emerging. A well-documented aspect of this is the shift from survival values to self-expression values, which has brought growing emphasis on human rights, tolerance of outgroups, environmental protection, gender equality, and freedom of expression (R. Inglehart, 1997; R. Inglehart & Norris, 2011; R. Inglehart & Welzel, 2005; R. F. Inglehart, 2018). Emphasis on these new norms has become widespread enough to evoke complaints about people being forced to comply with "political correctness."

Has the Shift toward Individual-Choice Norms Gone Too Far?

Survival is a balancing act. One can get too much—or too little—of almost anything needed for survival. In the 1970s, there was widespread concern that people were having too many children, producing a "population bomb" that would bring about mass starvation (Ehrlich et al., 1971). Although those fears proved unfounded, there is no question that birth rates can be too high: GDP per capita has both a numerator and a denominator, and if a country's population grows as fast as its output, the country will never escape poverty. For that reason, countries as diverse as communist China and theocratic Iran adopted antinatalist policies designed to reduce the birth rate.

Recent decades have brought the opposite concern—that people are having too few children to replace the population, making the welfare state unsustainable and resulting in inward-looking, less dynamic societies. Figure 9.5 shows that since 1950, the world's human fertility rates have dropped, from about 5.0 children per woman to slightly more than 2.5 children per woman. Almost half of the world's population now lives in countries with below-replacement fertility levels, and virtually all high-income countries now have fertility rates that are well below the population-replacement level of 2.1 children per woman.[3] The fertility rate for Europe as a whole fell from 2.66 in 1950 to 1.6 in 2015—a level so far below the population replacement level that it already is starting to bring population declines, and will bring much larger ones as the baby boom generation dies off. East Asia (China, Japan, North and South Korea, Taiwan, Hong Kong, and Mongolia) has experienced an even steeper decline than Europe, from a fertility rate of 5.56 in 1950 to 1.59 in 2015. This East Asian group is almost identical with the World Values Survey's Confucian-influenced cultural zone, except for the fact that Mongolia is only marginally Confucian- influenced, and, while geographically distant, Singapore

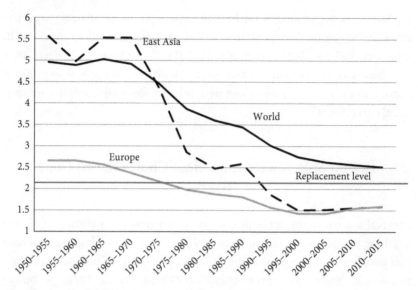

Figure 9.5 Total fertility rates in Europe, East Asia, and the world, 1950–2015. Vertical axis shows the expected number of children born per woman in her childbearing years.

Source: UN Population Division, 2017 World Population Prospects.

is largely Confucian-influenced and has shown a similar fertility decline, reaching a level of 1.23 children per woman in 2015. Unless these below-replacement fertility levels are offset by immigration, a steep population decline for the entire Confucian-influenced group is likely.

The world as a whole still has more people with traditional religious views than ever before because of higher birth rates in religious countries, but the difference is shrinking. Figure 9.6 shows the pattern for the U.S., Sweden, and France—three countries that had steep fertility declines from 1950 to the 1980s but then stabilized. In the U.S. until very recently, a low fertility rate among the U.S.-born population was offset by higher rates among recent immigrants, but in 2015 the U.S. rate fell to 1.88, continuing down to 1.73 in 2018. Since 2015, both France and Sweden have had higher fertility rates than the U.S. This can be traced back to the fact that, starting in the 1980s, France and Sweden adopted effective policies designed to encourage higher birth rates. In Sweden this reflected the country's high level of gender equality and its strong feminist movement (47 percent of

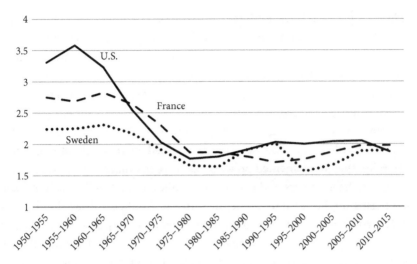

Figure 9.6 Total fertility rates in the U.S., France, and Sweden, 1950–2015. Vertical axis shows the expected number of children born per woman in her childbearing years.

Source: UN Population Division, 2017 World Population Prospects.

Swedish parliament members are women). Sweden and the other Nordic countries established a wide range of family-friendly initiatives, such as flexible working hours, an extensive network of affordable daycare centers, and generous parental leave systems that brought their birth rates close to the 2.1 population replacement level.

France has a long tradition of government policies designed to encourage higher birth rates, having had relatively low fertility rates throughout the 19th century. Since this meant that France was producing fewer military-age men than Germany, French governments provided cash incentives for additional children—but since the payments covered only a fraction of the actual cost of having children, they were not effective. But in the wake of the cultural changes of the 1970s, France adopted policies similar to, and in some ways even broader than, those of the Nordic countries. Both France and the Nordic countries offered young families cash and tax credits as incentives for having more children, but they also created extensive networks of almost-free kindergarten and infant schools and lengthy parental leaves, which in Sweden can last up to 480 days. Sweden's maternity-leave and paternity-leave policies are among the most generous in the world. Couples are required to split their parental leave, both fathers and mothers taking time off to spend with their children, and it has become frowned upon for fathers *not* to take their paternity leave. This means that employers have less incentive to promote men rather than women, since women are no longer much likelier than men to interrupt their careers when they have children. This enables women to have children and return to the labor force with good career prospects.

When women first began entering the work force, it had a negative impact on fertility rates. But as women attained increasingly strong political roles, they implemented policies like Sweden's that made it possible for women to have careers *and* two or more children. Left to themselves, male politicians might not have come up with these policies. They do not produce fertility rates of five children per woman, but they do enable societies to maintain population-replacement fertility levels. Since the 1980s, France and the Nordic countries have consistently had birth rates close to the replacement level, sometimes rising above it under favorable conditions and never falling far below it. Since the 2008 recession, birth rates have fallen throughout Europe, but these countries still have fertility rates well above the European average, with France and Sweden ranking first and second in the European Union.

From 1950 to 1985, the Nordic countries' fertility rates were well below those of southern Europe, but the situation then reversed itself, with historically Catholic nations, where contraceptives were once stigmatized or illegal, now recording some of the world's lowest levels. Italy's fertility rate is down to 1.34 per woman, Spain's is 1.30, Poland's is 1.33, and Portugal's is 1.28. As a result, their future ability to cover pensions and medical care for the old is becoming uncertain, and their populations are starting to decline. In these countries, religiosity has largely lost its power to control people's behavior, but feminist forces are still too weak to implement anything like the family-friendly policies of the Nordic countries and France.

Fertility rates in the Confucian-influenced countries of East Asia have fallen even lower than in Europe.[4] In 1979 China adopted a one-child-per-family policy, which undoubtedly helped reduce the country's fertility rate, but its impact tends to be overestimated: the effect of membership in the Confucian cultural zone seems to be at least equally important. China's fertility rate began to decline well before the one-child-per-family policy was adopted, and, as Figure 9.7 demonstrates, most of the other Confucian-influenced societies have even lower fertility rates than China's—without one-child-per-family policies. Today, in Confucian-influenced societies

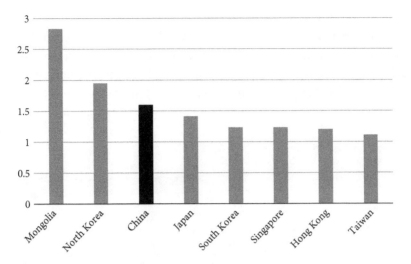

Figure 9.7 Fertility rates in Confucian-influenced countries (number of children born per woman of childbearing years, 2010–5)
Source: UN Population Division, 2017 World Population Prospects.

(and in historically Catholic societies), feminist forces are still too weak to cause the adoption of policies that might bring a return to replacement-level fertility rates (see Schoppa, 2010; cf. Goldscheider et al., 2010).

The Immigration Solution

The most obvious way of solving the problems of declining fertility would be through immigration. If people were purely rational, this would provide a quick and easy solution. But people have emotions, and the people who vote for xenophobic, authoritarian, populist parties are experiencing genuine stress and anxiety. Unless a country's rate of immigration is balanced against its socioeconomic context, cultural backlash tends to occur.[5]

In 2015, Angela Merkel courageously opened Germany's borders to all asylum-seekers. From a human rights perspective, this was admirable. But this gesture is now widely regarded as having damaged the cause of immigration, enabling the anti-immigrant Alternative for Germany to rise from obscurity to become Germany's third-largest party. Germany has subsequently cut back on immigration, and no other European government seems likely to follow Merkel's example.

Moreover, the numbers of immigrants that would be required to arrest Europe's population decline would be very large—dwarfing even the one million immigrants admitted to Germany in 2015. Immigration is part of the solution, but it is not a panacea. Successful politics demands more than ideological purity; it requires a careful balancing act that takes human emotions into account.

10

What Comes Next?

Rising existential security and the cultural changes linked with modernization bring declining emphasis on religion—and in high-income societies,
this process has reached a tipping point at which secularization accelerates.
Virtually all major world religions instill pro-fertility norms, but these norms
are rapidly giving way to individual-choice norms—and moving away from
religion.

The rapid erosion of pro-fertility norms is not the only factor driving secularization. Reactions against leading fundamentalists' unconditional support for xenophobic authoritarian politicians, against the Roman Catholic
Church's long history of covering up child abuse, and against terrorism by
religious extremists, all seem to be contributing to secularization.

Thus, as recently as 2019 a grand jury uncovered decades of sexual abuse
and cover-ups by Roman Catholic leaders, and the former archbishop of
Washington, D.C., Cardinal Theodore McCarrick, was forced to resign.
A 2020 Pew Research Center survey found that fully 92 percent of U.S. adults
had heard recent reports of sexual abuse by Catholic priests, and about
80 percent of them said that this reflected "ongoing problems that are still
happening" in the church. In addition, 27 percent of U.S. Catholics said that
they have scaled back attendance at Mass in response to reports of sexual
abuse (Pew Research Center, 2020).

On another front, terrorism by religious extremists evokes widespread disapproval—including in Muslim-majority countries. In 2008, a
BBC survey found (not surprisingly) that the publics of European, North
American, Latin American, African, and Asian countries had overwhelm-
ingly negative attitudes toward Al-Qaeda. Less obviously, the publics of
such Muslim-majority countries as Turkey, Egypt, Lebanon, and Indonesia
also had predominantly negative attitudes toward Al-Qaeda: 35 percent of
the Indonesians expressed negative feelings versus 16 percent with positive feelings; similarly, 36 percent of Egyptians expressed negative feelings,

Religion's Sudden Decline. Ronald F. Inglehart, Oxford University Press (2021). © Oxford University Press.
DOI: 10.1093/oso/9780197547045.003.0010

against 20 percent with positive feelings; 82 percent of Turks expressed negative feelings, and only 2 percent had positive feelings. Among Muslim-majority countries, only in Pakistan were feelings toward Al-Qaeda evenly divided, with 19 percent positive and 19 percent negative—and a majority were mixed or uncertain (BBC, 2008). In 2013, a Pew survey found that solid majorities of the publics in 10 of the 11 Muslim-majority countries covered said that "suicide bombings in defense of Islam" were rarely or never justified, with the majorities opposing them ranging from 58 percent (in Afghanistan) to 92 percent (in Indonesia). Only in the Palestine territory was opinion relatively divided, and even there 49 percent said it was rarely or never justified, while 40 percent said it was often or sometimes justified (Pew Research Center, September 10, 2013). One reason for this overwhelming disapproval of "suicide bombings in defense of Islam" is the fact that nearly 80 percent of the world's terrorism victims are Muslims. Between 2002 and 2018, the Middle East, South Asia, and sub-Saharan Africa accounted for 93 percent of all deaths from terrorism (TRT World, 2019). A negative reaction to religiously motivated terrorism has become another factor undermining support for religion.

Starting in the 1990s, the Republican Party in the U.S. sought to win new support by adopting the Christian conservative focus on sexual morality and opposition to same-sex marriage and abortion. Hout and Fischer (2002) argued that this didn't just attract religious voters; it also drove social liberals, especially young ones, away from religion. Initially, this claim seemed dubious because previous findings indicted that religion shapes one's political views, and not the other way around. But as religion weakens, the dominant causal flow can change direction, with religion shaping politics. Thus, using panel data, Hout and Fischer (2014) later found that people were not becoming more secular and then moving toward liberal politics; the main causal direction ran from politics to religion. One consequence was that from 1987 to 2012, the proportion of American adults who claimed no religious preference almost tripled, climbing from 7 to 20 percent of the population. Growing emphasis on personal autonomy largely explained why younger respondents were disproportionately likely to desert the Republican Party.

Many white evangelical Christians feel they have been mocked and patronized by the elite culture for decades. They see Trump as someone who will not only uphold their views on the courts and abortion but will be ruthless against people they see as destroying everything they know and love. As

Jerry Falwell Jr., the president of Liberty University, put it, "Conservatives and Christians need to stop electing 'nice guys.' . . . The United States needs street fighters like @realDonaldTrump at every level of government, because the liberal fascist Dems are playing for keeps." But the blatant hypocrisy of religious leaders who once made moral character and sexual fidelity central to their politics, and who are now embracing a massively corrupt leader, has costs. One prominent evangelist lamented the effect this is having, especially on younger people: "We're losing an entire generation. They're just gone. It's one of the worst things to happen to the Church" (cited in Wehner, 2019).

The Republican Party's current leaders may be making the same mistake. Although such prominent figures as Mitt Romney, George H. W. Bush, and George W. Bush have refused to back Trump, most of the party's top officeholders have been intimidated into following him down a path that is likely to exact heavy costs in support among the younger generation.

The accelerated recent decline of religion can't be attributed to any one cause. We will probably be unraveling its origins for some time. The causes include the three factors just discussed and unique nation-specific factors. But the reversal of the causal flow between religion and pro-fertility norms seems to be a particularly pervasive and widely underestimated influence. Throughout most of recorded history, religion was able to impose pro-fertility norms. In recent decades, rising support for individual-choice norms has been undermining support for religion. As we have seen, this factor explains a large share (though by no means all) of the cross-national and cross-temporal variation in religiosity.

Rapid cultural changes, exacerbated by economic distress, have triggered a powerful authoritarian reflex, and we are witnessing a democratic recession, not only in countries that never had deep-rooted democratic political cultures but even in established democracies such as the U.S., Britain, France, Germany, and the Nordic countries. Is this the wave of the future? It largely depends on whether developed countries learn to cope with advanced knowledge societies' inherent tendency to have winner-takes-all economies. Left to market forces, these countries will continue to experience rapidly rising economic inequality and diminishing existential security for a growing share of the population. The 2020 coronavirus pandemic may be encouraging support for radical change. A March 2020 survey of the publics of the 27 European Union countries found that fully 71 percent of the respondents were in favor of introducing a universal basic income—a position once widely regarded as utopian (Ash & Zimmerman, 2020).

It also depends on striking a balance between a healthy openness to immigration and allowing such rapid demographic change that older generations feel they have become strangers in their own land. Stigmatizing these people as bigots will not solve the problem. Meeting this challenge will require experimentation and innovation.

The Covid-19 pandemic poses another threat to people's sense of existential security. If this threat prevails for decades (as seems unlikely), it could reshape cultures, making them more xenophobic and closed to new ideas. Several important empirical studies have shown that societies that are vulnerable to disease tend to have authoritarian and xenophobic cultures and institutions (Chiao & Blizinsky, 2009; Fincher et al., 2008; Gelfand et al., 2011; Thornhill et al., 2010), and the coronavirus poses the most serious disease-linked threat in more than a century.

But the triumph of the authoritarian reflex is not inevitable. The established democracies have just transitioned from a world in which religiosity and pro-fertility norms were socially dominant to one in which religiosity and traditional norms have minority status. This exceptionally rapid cultural change, combined with an exceptionally large influx of foreigners, has evoked strong negative reactions. But as older birth cohorts are replaced by younger ones that have grown up under the new conditions, the intensity of the authoritarian reaction is likely to diminish. In the long run, scientific and technological progress tends to induce rising levels of existential security—and they will do so if appropriate policies are adopted to cope with the immediate challenge of the coronavirus and the enduring problem of rising inequality that is inherent in advanced knowledge societies.

But the triumph of the Authoritarian Reflex is not inevitable. The established democracies have just transitioned from a world in which religiosity and Pro-fertility norms were socially dominant, to one in which religiosity and traditional norms have minority status. This exceptionally rapid cultural change, combined with an exceptionally large influx of foreigners, has evoked strong negative reactions. But as older birth cohorts are replaced by younger ones that have grown up under the new conditions, the intensity of the authoritarian reaction is likely to diminish. In the long run, scientific and technological progress tend to bring rising levels of existential security—and they will do so if appropriate policies are adopted to cope with the immediate challenges of the coronavirus, and the enduring problem of rising inequality that is inherent in advanced knowledge societies. But for the immediate future, we would expect the insecurities linked with the pandemic to generate support for religion. The Aggregate Religiosity Index of Figure 7.10 showed a sharp decline in recent years. If it were measured again for the year 2020, we would expect it to show an upward turn.

God as a Work in Progress

Humans have evolved to seek meaningful patterns; birds chattering in the trees, for instance, might signal the approach of a predator. Being able to predict what might happen was conducive to survival. Eventually, the search for meaningful patterns expanded to seeking to know the meaning of life itself.

But is the universe meaningful, or is the search for meaning a delusion? The answer is not yet in, because meaning is an evolving phenomenon. For the first four billion years of this planet's existence, there was no sentient life. Good and evil, truth and lies, were meaningless concepts. Reading them back into the past *is* illusory. Teilhard de Chardin (1959) views the universe as incomplete, with both human society and God still being constructed. From this perspective, we are creating God.

Since biblical times, concepts of God have evolved from a merciless tribal God who demanded human sacrifice to a benevolent God whose laws apply to everyone. Moral concepts are also evolving, with declining racism, sexism, and homophobia reflecting a trend away from inward-looking tribal norms that excluded most of humanity, toward universal moral norms. As societies develop from agrarian to industrial to knowledge societies, growing existential security reduces the importance of traditional religion in people's lives, and people become less obedient to traditional religious leaders and institutions. But they don't become amoral.

We have free will, and it hangs in the balance whether the emergence of intelligent life in the universe turns out to be a tale told by an idiot or one in which we will become a little lower than the angels. The balance could be so close that everyone's contribution matters.

Traditional religions can be dangerously divisive in contemporary global society because they present each culture's norms as absolute, universal values. But a massive body of evidence indicates that any society's cultural patterns are closely linked with its history and socioeconomic characteristics. The rigidity of any absolute belief system can give rise to fanatic intolerance, as the historical struggles between Protestant and Catholic and between

Christianity and Islam demonstrate. To function positively in a globalizing world, religion needs a universal perspective.

The possibility of life and God are built into the structure of the universe. It is possible that the emergence of intelligent life could turn out to be a cruel joke. Sadistic monsters like Hitler and Stalin are possible. And Mother Teresa and Albert Schweitzer—and some less famous people whom I've known personally—show that the opposite is also possible. We have a wide range of choice, and how it ends depends on us: we can help decide the ultimate meaning of the universe. The reality can turn out to be even nobler than Michelangelo's Sistine Chapel image of God creating Adam.

The cosmology of the Big Bang is at least as impressive as the account in Genesis. It is awe-inspiring that human intelligence has been able to penetrate back to the first few minutes of the universe's existence. That universe had the potential to develop good and evil, benevolence and meaning— but none of these things existed before intelligent life emerged. From this perspective, the account of creation in the book of Genesis can be seen as a first approximation of the more recent account provided by the Big Bang theory—which is only a first approximation of the ultimate account. Both traditional religion and modern science provide successive approximations of a truth that is still being fathomed. The search for meaning will continue.

Appendix

Table A.1. Predicting religiosity: Results of a three-level model

	Estimate
Individual level	
Individual-choice values	−0.252***
	(0.001)
Country-year level	
Individual-choice values	−0.267***
	(0.045)
Time	0.080***
	(0.014)
Country level	
Log infant mortality 1980	0.146***
	(0.038)
Muslim tradition	−0.031
	(0.024)
Confucian tradition	−0.220***
	(0.041)
Communist rule after World War II	−0.131***
	(0.021)
Constant	0.772***
	(0.027)
Variance parameters	
Individual level	0.050
Country-year level	0.003
Country level	0.006
Observations	
Individual level	515,190
Country-year level	351
Country level	89

Note. Standard errors in parentheses.

* $p < .05$, ** $p < .01$, *** $p < .001$

Table A.2. Mean scores on individual-choice norms in high-income societies (countries
that the World Bank classified as "high income" in 2000)

Andorra (2005)	7.96	**France (2018)**	**6.93**
Andorra (2018)	**7.44**	Germany (1990)	4.77
Australia (1981)	4.38	Germany (1997)	7.91
Australia (1995)	5.13	Germany (1999)	5.41
Australia (2005)	5.99	Germany (2008)	5.47
Australia (2012)	6.58	**Germany (2017)**	**7.17**
Australia (2018)	**7.21**	Greece (1999)	5.40
Austria (1990)	4.00	Greece (2008)	4.65
Austria (1999)	5.32	Greece (2017)	5.36
Austria (2008)	5.31	Hong Kong (2005)	3.99
Austria (2018)	**6.78**	Hong Kong (2014)	3.99
Belgium (1981)	3.45	Hong Kong (2018)	4.65
Belgium (1990)	4.45	Iceland (1984)	4.35
Belgium (1999)	5.07	Iceland (1990)	5.53
Belgium (2009)	5.47	Iceland (1999)	6.41
Canada (1982)	3.89	Iceland (2009)	7.24
Canada (1990)	4.85	**Iceland (2017)**	**8.15**
Canada (2000)	5.39	Ireland (1981)	2.52
Canada (2006)	5.44	Ireland (1990)	3.22
Denmark (1981)	6.16	Ireland (1999)	3.96
Denmark (1999)	6.99	Ireland (2008)	4.58
Denmark (2008)	7.49	Italy (1981)	3.97
Denmark (2017)	**8.57**	Italy (1990)	4.36
Finland (1981)	4.63	Italy (1999)	4.67
Finland (1990)	6.05	Italy (2005)	3.94
Finland (1996)	5.42	**Italy (2018)**	**5.91**
Finland (2000)	5.68	Japan (1981)	3.50
Finland (2005)	6.08	Japan (1990)	3.69
Finland (2009)	6.72	Japan (1995)	4.51
Finland (2017)	**7.35**	Japan (2000)	5.15
France (1981)	4.45	Japan (2005)	5.27
France (1990)	4.86	Japan (2010)	5.34
France (1999)	5.75	**Japan (2019)**	**6.13**
France (2006)	6.61	Luxembourg (1999)	5.75
France (2008)	6.12	Luxembourg (2008)	5.94

Table A.2.. *Continued*

Netherlands (1981)	4.93	Spain (2011)	6.73
Netherlands (1990)	6.20	**Spain (2017)**	**6.79**
Netherlands (1999)	6.65	Sweden (1981)	5.38
Netherlands (2006)	6.40	Sweden (1982)	5.32
Netherlands (2008)	6.53	Sweden (1990)	5.42
Netherlands (2012)	7.26	Sweden (1996)	7.31
Netherlands (2017)	**7.78**	Sweden (1999)	7.61
New Zealand (1998)	5.39	Sweden (2006)	8.24
New Zealand (2004)	5.80	Sweden (2009)	7.96
New Zealand (2011)	**5.92**	Sweden (2011)	8.11
Norway (1982)	4.50	**Sweden (2017)**	**8.49**
Norway (1990)	4.83	Switzerland (1989)	4.09
Norway (1996)	5.75	Switzerland (1996)	5.96
Norway (2007)	7.24	Switzerland (2007)	6.61
Norway (2008)	6.78	Switzerland (2008)	5.92
Norway (2018)	**7.96**	**Switzerland (2017)**	**7.17**
Portugal (1990)	3.97	Great Britain (1981)	4.14
Portugal (1999)	4.13	Great Britain (1990)	4.44
Portugal (2008)	4.95	Great Britain (1998)	5.72
Slovenia (1992)	5.31	Great Britain (1999)	5.01
Slovenia (1995)	5.21	Great Britain (2005)	5.71
Slovenia (1999)	5.80	Great Britain (2009)	5.45
Slovenia (2005)	6.23	**Great Britain (2018)**	**6.90**
Slovenia (2008)	5.41	U.S. (1982)	3.49
Slovenia (2011)	6.49	U.S. (1990)	3.98
Slovenia (2017)	6.58	U.S. (1995)	4.34
Spain (1981)	3.44	U.S. (1999)	5.02
Spain (1990)	4.56	U.S. (2006)	4.97
Spain (1995)	5.36	U.S. (2011)	5.48
Spain (1999)	5.35	**U.S. (2017)**	**5.86**
Spain (2000)	5.83	**West Germany (1981)**	**4.13**
Spain (2007)	6.46	**West Germany 2017**	**6.24**
Spain (2008)	5.99	**East Germany 2017**	**6.01**

Table A.3. Countries ranked by religiosity in quintiles, as indicated by mean score on "Importance of God in one's life" in latest available survey

1st (least religious) quintile	Russia (2017)	Lebanon (2018)
Australia (2012)	Serbia (2017)	Mali (2007)
Belgium (2009)	Slovakia (2008)	Malta (2008)
China (2013)	Switzerland (2008)	Mexico (2012)
Czech Republic (2008)	Taiwan (2012)	Nigeria (2018)
Denmark (2008)	Uruguay (2011)	Peru (2012)
Estonia (2011)	**3rd quintile**	Philippines (2012)
France (2008)	Albania (2008)	Romania (2018)
Germany (2018)	Argentina (2017)	Turkey (2012)
Hong Kong (2014)	Armenia (2011)	Uganda (2001)
Japan (2010)	Canada (2006)	Uzbekistan (2011)
Luxembourg (2008)	Croatia (2008)	Zambia (2007)
Netherlands (2012)	Greece (2017)	**5th (most religious) quintile**
Norway (2008)	Haiti (2016)	Algeria (2014)
South Korea (2018)	India (2012)	Azerbaijan (2011)
Slovenia (2011)	Israel (2001)	Bangladesh (2002)
Spain (2011)	Italy (2009)	Colombia (2012)
Sweden (2011)	Kazakhstan (2011)	Egypt (2018)
Thailand (2018)	Kyrgyzstan (2011)	El Salvador (1999)
United Kingdom (2009)	Macedonia (2008)	Ghana (2012)
United States (2017)	Malaysia (2018)	Guatemala (2004)
Vietnam (2006)	Moldova (2008)	Indonesia (2006)
2nd quintile	Montenegro (2008)	Jordan (2018)
Andorra (2005)	Poland (2017)	Libya (2014)
Austria (2008)	Rwanda (2012)	Morocco (2011)
Belarus (2011)	Singapore (2012)	Pakistan (2012)
Bulgaria (2008)	South Africa (2013)	Puerto Rico (2001)
Chile (2018)	Ukraine (2011)	Qatar (2010)
Finland (2009)	**4th quintile**	Saudi Arabia (2003)
Hungary (2009)	Bolivia (2017)	Tanzania (2001)
Iceland (2009)	Brazil (2014)	Trinidad (2010)
Ireland (2008)	Burkina Faso (2007)	Tunisia (2013)
Latvia (2008)	Cyprus (2011)	Venezuela (2000)
Lithuania (2008)	Ecuador (2018)	Yemen (2014)
New Zealand (2011)	Ethiopia (2007)	Zimbabwe (2012)
Northern Ireland (2008)	Georgia (2014)	
Portugal (2008)	Kosovo (2008)	

Notes

Preface

1. In early 2020, the coronavirus pandemic interrupted the most recent wave of surveys, suspending data collection in an additional 25 countries for an uncertain period of time.

Chapter 1

1. To focus on enduring changes rather than short-term fluctuations, a minimum time series of 15 years was required for inclusion in this analysis; the median time span was almost 20 years.
2. These figures are based on the pooled data from all surveys of high-income countries included in the WVS and EVS.
3. Factor analysis indicates that this item is the most sensitive indicator of a broad underlying religiosity factor among more than 20 variables.

Chapter 2

1. China Family Panel Study 2012 survey, *The World Religious Cultures* issue 2014.
2. For greater detail on how the two dimensions were constructed, see R. Inglehart, 1997, Chapter 1.

Chapter 3

1. This is computed as the sum of squares of the proportions of each denomination within a given country or region; see Chaves & Cann, 1992; Halman & Draulans, 2006; McCleary & Barro, 2006; Smith et al., 1998.
2. For a discussion of the comparative evidence, see Bok, 1996.

Chapter 4

1. Based on the World Bank's classifications in 2000, the low-income countries had a mean per capita income of $1,582 (purchasing power parity estimates) and a mean infant mortality rate of 54.5; these figures rise as we move through the middle-income

countries. Among the high-income countries the mean per capita income was $27,223 and mean infant mortality was 4.4.

Chapter 5

1. Three publics showed no change.

Chapter 6

1. The World Bank does not provide complete data on real GDP per capita before 1990 because many of these countries did not exist as independent countries before the collapse of communism around 1990.
2. The dependent variable is a three-item index based on the subjective importance of religion, self-identification as religious or nonreligious, and religious participation.

Chapter 7

1. This scale reflects the mean of each country's scores on the three 10-point scales measuring acceptance of (1) divorce, (2) abortion, and (3) homosexuality.
2. If the scale ran from 0 to 10, the midpoint would be 5, but it runs from 1 to 10.
3. The number of respondents in the two respective groups is 1,225 and 3,199.

Chapter 8

1. This apology is heartfelt: I was a student and later a visiting professor at Leiden University and have a Dutch daughter.
2. Piketty's data sources are available on his page at the website of the Paris School of Economics, http://piketty.pse.ens.fr/capital21c.
3. Today, Switzerland and the Netherlands have more practicing Catholics than Protestants, but their cultures reflect their historical heritage rather than their contemporary church attendance, and both countries were historically dominated by Protestantism.
4. Religious people may also be relatively likely to agree with survey statements. The Schwartz battery asks "Now I will briefly describe some people. Would you please indicate for each description whether that person is very much like you, like you, somewhat like you, not like you, or not at all like you?" Nationalities that score high on religiosity on the religious/individual-choice index are much likelier to say that the person described on all 10 of Schwartz's values battery is very much like themselves, although some of the items contradict each other. For example, people who emphasize religion are much likelier than people who emphasize individual choice to say that they are very much like a person who takes risks and that they are very much like a person who avoids anything that might be dangerous.

5. For complete information on the methodology, see Freedom House, n.d.

6. Life satisfaction was assessed by asking respondents how satisfied they were with their lives as a whole, using a scale ranging from 1, "not at all satisfied," to 10, "very satisfied." Happiness was assessed by asking respondents to indicate how happy they were, using four categories: "very happy," "rather happy," "not very happy," and "not at all happy." The economic data is from the World Bank.

7. Among those who said that homosexuality is never justifiable, 25 percent said they were very happy; among those who said it was always justifiable, 31 percent were very happy.

Chapter 9

1. The coronavirus pandemic is unusual in one important respect: it has imposed massive quarantines, isolating people from others for long periods of time—making human contact scarce and increasingly valuable and generating a tendency to reach out to others.

2. For Italy, see DEMOS surveys of Conte; for France, Ipsos surveys of Macron; for Germany, Forschungsgruppe Wahlen surveys of Merkel; for U.S., Gallup surveys of Trump. Also see the Twitter feed of Leonardo Carella, https://twitter.com/leonardocarella/status/1243648800872443904.

3. It would be 2.0 except for the fact that not all children survive to reach the age of reproduction.

4. This may be an indication that religious incentives for high fertility rates are more enduring than secular ones.

5. For a detailed discussion of this problem, see Norris and Inglehart, 2019.

Bibliography

Aikman, D. (2003). *The Beijing factor: How Christianity is transforming China and changing the global balance of power.*

Aldridge, A. (2000). *Religion in the contemporary world.* Polity Press.

Alexander, A. C., Inglehart, R., & Welzel, C. (2016). Emancipating sexuality: Breakthroughs into a bulwark of tradition. *Social Indicators Research, 129*(2), 909–35.

Alimujiang, A., Wiensch, A., Boss, J., Fleischer, N. L., Mondul, A. M., McLean, K., & Pearce, C. L. (2019). Association between life purpose and mortality among US adults older than 50 years. *JAMA Network Open, 2*(5), e194270–e194270.

Andersen, R., & Fetner, T. (2008). Cohort differences in tolerance of homosexuality. *Public Opinion Quarterly, 72*(2), 311–30.

Armstrong, K. (2001). *The battle for God.* Ballantine Books.

Asad, T. (2003). *Formations of the secular: Christianity, Islam, modernity.* Stanford University Press.

Ash, T. G., & Zimmermann, A. (2020, May 6). *In crisis, Europeans support radical positions.* Eupinions. https://eupinions.eu/de/text/in-crisis-europeans-support-radical-positions

Baril, A., & Mori, G. A. (1991, Autumn). Leaving the fold: Declining church attendance. *Canadian Social Trends*, pp. 21–4.

Barro, R. J. (1997). *Determinants of economic growth: A cross-country empirical study.* MIT Press.

Barro, R. J., & McCleary, R. M. (2003). Religion and economic growth across countries. *American Sociological Review, 68*(5),760–81.

Barro, R. J., & McCleary, R. M. (2009). Religion and political economy in an international panel. In S. Becker & L. Wössmann (Eds.), Was Weber wrong? A human capital theory of Protestant economic history [Special issue]. *Quarterly Journal of Economics, 124*(2), 531–96.

Barro, R. J., & McCleary, R. (2019). *The wealth of religions: The political economy of believing and belonging.* Princeton University Press.

BBC Survey September, 2008. (2008). http://news.bbc.co.uk/2/hi/americas/7638566.stm

Benda, B. B., & Toombs, N. J. (2000). Religiosity and violence: Are they related after considering the strongest predictors? *Journal of Criminal Justice, 28*(6), 483–96.

Berger, P. L. (1967). *The sacred canopy: Elements of a sociological theory of religion.* Doubleday.

Berger, P. L. (1992). *A far glory: The quest for faith in an age of credulity.* Anchor.

Bibby, R. W. (1979). The state of collective religiosity in Canada: An empirical analysis. *Canadian Review of Sociology and Anthropology, 16*(1), 105–16,

Bok, D. (1996). *The state of the nation: Government and the quest for a better society.* Harvard University Press.

Brader, T., Valentino, N. A., & Suhay, E. (2008). What triggers public opposition to immigration? Anxiety, group cues, and immigration threat. *American Journal of Political Science, 52*(4), 959–78.

Broadberry, S., & O'Rourke, K. (Eds.). (2010). *The Cambridge economic history of modern Europe: 1700–1870.* Cambridge University Press.

Bruce, S. (1992). Pluralism and religious vitality. In S. Bruce (Ed.), *Religion and modernization: Sociologists and historians debate the secularization thesis* (pp. 000–000). Oxford University Press.

Bruce, S. (2002). *God is dead: Secularization in the West.* Blackwell.

Bushman, B. J., Ridge, R. D., Das, E., Key, C. W., & Busath, G. L. (2007). When God sanctions killing: Effect of scriptural violence on aggression. *Psychological Science, 18*(3), 204–7.

Caluori, N., Jackson, J. C., Gray, K., & Gelfand, M. (2020). Conflict changes how people view God. *Psychological Science, 31*(3), 280–92.

Carter, A. (2012). *People power and political change.* Routledge.

Casanova, J. (1994). *Public religions in the modern world.* University of Chicago Press.

Case, A., & Deaton, A. (2020). The epidemic of despair: Will America's mortality crisis spread to the rest of the world? *Foreign Affairs, 99*(2), 92–102.

Chaves, M., & Cann, D. E. (1992). Regulation, pluralism, and religious market structure: Explaining religion's vitality. *Rationality and Society, 4*(3), 272–90.

Chaves, M., & Gorski, P. S. (2001). Religious pluralism and religious participation. *Annual Review of Sociology, 27,* 261–81.

Chiao, J. Y., & Blizinsky, K. D. (2009). Culture-gene coevolution of individualism-collectivism and the serotonin transporter gene. *Proceedings of the Royal Society B, 277*(1681), 529–53.

Chludzinski, J. (2020). *The interplay of religion and the economy: Has religion impacted economic development?* [Unpublished honors thesis]. University of Michigan.

CIA. (2019). *The world factbook.* https://www.cia.gov/library/publications/the-world-factbook/rankorder/2172rank.html

Clark, H. (2009). *People power.* Pluto Press.

Datler, G., Jagodzinski, W., & Schmidt, P. (2013). Two theories on the test bench: Internal and external validity of the theories of Ronald Inglehart and Shalom Schwartz. *Social Science Research, 42*(3), 906–25.

Davie, G. (2002). *Europe: The exceptional case: Parameters of faith in the modern world.* Dartan, Longman, and Todd.

Dawkins, R. (1977). *The selfish gene.* Oxford University Press.

Di Prete, T. A., & Eirich, G. M. (2006). Cumulative advantage as a mechanism for inequality: A review of theoretical and empirical developments. *Annual Review of Sociology, 32,* 271–97.

Diamond, J. M. (2013). *The world until yesterday: What can we learn from traditional societies?* Penguin.

Dobbelaere, K. (1987). Some trends in European sociology of religion: The secularization debate. *Sociological Analysis, 48,* 107–13.

Dobbelaere, K. (2002). *Secularization: An analysis at three levels* (Vol. 1). Peter Lang.

Duckitt, J., & Bizumic, B. (2013). Multidimensionality of right-wing authoritarian attitudes: Authoritarianism-conservatism-traditionalism. *Political Psychology, 34*(6), 841–62.

Duckitt, J., Bizumic, B., Krauss, S. W., & Heled, E. (2010). A tripartite approach to right-wing authoritarianism: The authoritarianism-conservatism-traditionalism model. *Political Psychology, 31*(5), 685–715.

Durkheim, E. 1995. *The elementary forms of the religious life.* Free Press. (Original work published 1912)

Economy, E. C. (2018). *The third revolution: Xi Jinping and the new Chinese state.* Oxford University Press.

Ehrlich, P. R., Parnell, D., & Silbowitz, A. (1971). *The population bomb.* Ballantine Books.

FactsMaps. (2018). *PISA 2018 worldwide ranking: Average score of mathematics, science and reading.* http://factsmaps.com/pisa-2018-worldwide-ranking-average-score-of-mathematics-science-reading/

Ferguson, N. (2012). *Civilization: The West and the rest.* Penguin.

Fincher, C. L., Thornhill, R., Murray, D. R., & Schaller, M. (2008). Pathogen prevalence predicts human cross-cultural variability in individualism/collectivism. *Proceedings of the Royal Society B, 275*(1640), 1279–85.

Finke, R., & Iannaccone, L. R. (1993, May). Supply-side explanations for religious change. *The Annals of the American Academy of Political and Social Sciences, 527,* 27–39.

Finke, R., & Stark, R. (1988). Religious economies and sacred canopies. *American Sociological Review, 53,* 41–9.

Frank, D. J., Camp, B. J., & Boutcher, S. A. (2010). Worldwide trends in the criminal regulation of sex, 1945 to 2005. *American Sociological Review, 75*(6), 867–93.

Freedom House. (n.d.). *Freedom in the world 2018 methodology.* https://freedomhouse.org/report/freedom-world-2018/methodology

Freedom House. (2019). *Freedom in the world.* https://freedomhouse.org/sites/default/files/Feb2019_FH_FITW_2019_Report_ForWeb-compressed.pdf

Galli, M. (2020, January 24). Evangelicals have a role in political life: It isn't fawning over Trump. *Los Angeles Times,* op-ed.

Gallup International. (2019). *2019 European Election Survey.* https://www.gallup-international.com/surveys/eu-future-brexit/

Gangestad, S. W., & Buss, D. M. (1993). Pathogen prevalence and human mate preferences. *Ethology and sociobiology, 14*(2), 89–96.

Gat, A. (2006). *War in human civilization.* Oxford University Press.

Gelfand, M. J., Raver, J. L., Nishii, L., Leslie, L. M., Lun, J., Lim, B. C., Duan, L., et al. (2011). Differences between tight and loose cultures: A 33-nation study. *Science, 332*(6033), 1100–4.

General Social Survey. (1972–2018). https://gss.norc.org/Get-The-Data

Gifford, P. (2019). *The plight of Western religion: The eclipse of the other-worldly.* C. Hurst and Company.

Goldscheider, F., Bernhardt, E., & Lappegård, T. (2015). The gender revolution: A framework for understanding changing family and demographic behavior. *Population and Development Review, 41*(2), 207–39.

Gorodzeisky, A., & Semyonov, M. (2016). Not only competitive threat but also racial prejudice: Sources of anti-immigrant attitudes in European societies. *International Journal of Public Opinion Research, 28*(3), 331–54.

Gorski, P. S., & Altınordu, A. (2008). After secularization? *Annual Review of Sociology, 34,* 55–85.

Grant, J. T. (2008). Measuring aggregate religiosity in the United States, 1952–2005. *Sociological Spectrum, 28*(5), 460–76.

Greeley, A. M. (1972). *Unsecular man: The persistence of religion.* Schocken.

Greeley, A. M. (2003). *Religion in Europe at the end of the second millennium.* Transaction.

Gustafsson, G. (1994). Religious change in the five Scandinavian countries, 1930–1980. In T. Pettersson & O. Riis (Eds.), *Scandinavian values: Religion and morality in the Nordic countries.* Acta Universitatis Upsaliensis.

Hadden, J. K. (1987). Toward desacralizing secularization theory. *Social Forces, 65,* 587–611.

Halman, L., & Draulans, V. (2006). How secular is Europe? *British Journal of Sociology, 57,* 263–88.

Hervieu-Léger, D. (2000). *Religion as a chain of memory.* Polity Press.

Hofstede, Geert. (2001). *Culture's consequences: Comparing values, behaviors, institutions and organizations across nations.* 2nd ed. Sage Publications.

Hogan, B. (2020, March 30). New Yorkers approve of Cuomo's response to coronavirus pandemic: Poll. *New York Post.*

Hout, M. & Fischer, C. S. (2002). Why more Americans have no religious preference: Politics and generations. *American Sociological Review, 67*(2), 165–90.

Hout, M., & Fischer, C. S. (2014). Explaining why more Americans have no religious preference: Political backlash and generational succession, 1987–2012. *Sociological Science, 1,* 423–47.

Hughes, B., & Hillebrand, E. (2012). *Exploring and shaping international futures.* Routledge.

Iannaccone, L. R. (1990). Religious practice: A human capital approach." *Journal for the Scientific Study of Religion, 29,* 297–314.

Iannaccone, L. R. (1991). The consequences of religious market structures: Adam Smith and the economics of religion. *Rationality and Society, 34*(2), 156–77.

Iannaccone, L. R. (1995). Voodoo economics? Reviewing the rational choice approach to religion. *Journal for the Scientific Study of Religion, 34,* 76–89.

Immerzeel, T., & van Tubergen, F. (2011). Religion as reassurance? Testing the insecurity theory in 26 European countries. *European Sociological Review, 29*(2), 359–72.

Index Mundi, n.d. *Intentional homicides (per 100,000 people): Country ranking.* https://www.indexmundi.com/facts/indicators/VC.IHR.PSRC.P5/rankings

Inglehart, R. (1977). *The silent revolution: Changing values and political styles among Western publics.* Princeton University Press.

Inglehart, R. (1997). *Modernization and postmodernization: Cultural, economic and political change in 43 societies.* Princeton University Press.

Inglehart, R., & Baker, W. E. (2000). Modernization, cultural change, and the persistence of traditional values. *American Sociological Review, 65*(1), 19–51.

Inglehart, R., Foa, R., Peterson, C., & Welzel, C. (2008). Development, freedom and rising happiness: A global perspective, 1981–2007. *Perspectives on Psychological Science, 3*(4), 264–85.

Inglehart, R., & Welzel, C. (2005). *Modernization, cultural change and democracy.* Cambridge University Press.

Inglehart, R., & Welzel, C. (2010). Changing mass priorities: The link between modernization and democracy. *Perspectives on Politics, 8*(2), 551–67.

Inglehart, R. F. (2018). *Cultural evolution: People's motivations are changing, and reshaping the world*. Cambridge University Press.

Jiwei, C. (1994). *Dialectic of the Chinese revolution*. Stanford University Press.

Lechner, F. J. (1996). Secularization in the Netherlands? *Journal of the Scientific Study of Religion, 35*, 252–64.

Liu, Z., Guo, Q., Sun, P., Wang, Z., & Wu, R. (2018). Does religion hinder creativity? A national level study on the roles of religiosity and different denominations. *Frontiers in Psychology, 9*, 1912.

Low, B. S. (1990). Marriage systems and pathogen stress in human societies. *American Zoologist, 30*(2), 325–40.

Luckmann, T. (1967). *The invisible religion: The problem of religion in modern society*. Macmillan.

Luckmann, T. (1991). *Die unsichtbare religion*. Suhrkamp.

Markoff, J. (1996). *Waves of democracy*. Pine Forge Press.

McAllister, I. (1988). Religious change and secularization: The transmission of religious values in Australia. *Sociological Analysis, 49*(3), 249–63.

McCleary, R. M., & Barro, R. J. (2006). Religion and economy. *Journal of Economic Perspectives, 20*(2), 49–72.

McCleary, R. M., & Barro, R. J. (2006). Religion and political economy in an international panel. *Journal for the Scientific Study of Religion, 45*, 149–75.

Michelat, G., et al. (1991). *Les français, sont-ils encore catholiques? Analyse d'un sondage d'opinion*. Editions du Cerf.

Milanovic, B. (2020). The clash of capitalisms: The real fight for the global economy's future. *Foreign Affairs, 99*(1), 10–21.

Miller, J. (2006). *Chinese religions in contemporary societies*. ABC-CLIO.

Mol, H. (1985). *The faith of Australians*. George, Allen, and Unwin.

Murray, D. R., Jones, D. N., & Schaller, M. (2013). Perceived threat of infectious disease and its implications for sexual attitudes. *Personality and Individual Differences, 54*(1), 103–8.

Murray, D. R., & Schaller, M. (2010). Historical prevalence of infectious diseases within 230 geopolitical regions: A tool for investigating origins of culture. *Journal of Cross-Cultural Psychology, 41*(1), 99–108.

Murray, D. R., & Schaller, M. (2012). Threat(s) and conformity deconstructed: Perceived threat of infectious disease and its implications for conformist attitudes and behavior. *European Journal of Social Psychology, 42*(2), 180–8.

Murray, D. R., Trudeau, R., & Schaller, M. (2011). On the origins of cultural differences in conformity: Four tests of the pathogen prevalence hypothesis. *Personality and Social Psychology Bulletin, 37*(3), 318–29.

Need, A., & De Graaf, N. D. (1996) Losing my religion: A dynamic analysis of leaving the church in the Netherlands." *European Sociological Review, 12*, 87–99.

Neuberg, S. L., Kenrick, D. T., & Schaller, M. (2011). Human threat management systems: Self-protection and disease avoidance. *Neuroscience and Biobehavioral Reviews, 35*(4), 1042–51.

Nolan, P., & Lenski, G. (2015). *Human societies: An introduction to macrosociology*. Oxford University Press.

Norris, P., & Inglehart, R. (2011). *Sacred and secular: Religion and politics worldwide*. Rev. 2nd ed. Cambridge University Press. (Original work published 2004)

OECD. (2017). *Financing for sustainable development*. http://www.oecd.org/dac/financing-sustainable-development/

Pettersson, T., & Hamberg, E. M. (1997). Denominational pluralism and church membership in contemporary Sweden: A longitudinal study of the period, 1974–1995. *Journal of Empirical Theology, 10*, 61–78.

Pew Research Center. 2013, April 30. Muslim publics share concerns about extremist groups.

Pew Research Center. 2019, October 17. In U.S., decline of Christianity continues at rapid pace.

Pew Research Center. 2019, November 15. Americans have positive views about religion's role in society, but want it out of politics.

Pew Research Center. 2020, April 18. *Americans see Catholic clergy sex abuse as an ongoing problem*.

Piketty, T. (2014). *Capital in the twenty-first century*. Harvard University Press.

Pinker, S. (2011). *The better angels of our nature*. Viking.

Pollack, D. (2009). A renaissance of religion? Findings of social research. *Osteuropa, 59*(6), 29–31.

Pollack, D., & Pickel, G. (2007). Religious individualization or secularization? Testing hypotheses of religious change—The case of Eastern and Western Germany. *The British Journal of Sociology, 58*(4), 603–32.

Prentice, T. (2006). Health, history and hard choices. *Nonprofit and Voluntary Sector Quarterly, 37*(1), 63S–75S.

Puranen, B. (2008). *How values transform military culture: The Swedish example*. Values Research Institute.

Puranen, B. (2009). European values on security and defence: An exploration of the correlates of willingness to fight for one's country. In Y. Esmer, H. D. Klingemann, & Bi Puranen (Eds.), *Religion, democratic values and political conflict* (pp. 277–304). Uppsala University.

Putnam, R. D., & Campbell, D. E. (2010). *American grace: How religion divides and unites us*.

Rapp-Hooper, M. (2020, March 24). China, America, and the international order after the pandemic. *Texas National Security Review*. https://warontherocks.com/2020/03/china-america-and-the-international-order-after-the-pandemic/

Ridley, M. (2012). The rational optimist: How prosperity evolves. *Brock Education: A Journal of Educational Research and Practice, 21*(2), 103–6.

Roof, W. C. (1993). *A generation of seekers: The spiritual journeys of the baby boom generation*. HarperCollins.

Roof, W. C. (2001). *Spiritual marketplace: Baby-boomers and the remaking of American religion*. Princeton University Press.

Ruiter, S., & van Tubergen, F. (2009). Religious attendance in cross-national perspective: A multilevel analysis of 60 countries. *American Journal of Sociology, 115*(3), 863–95.

Schoppa, L. (2010). Exit, voice, and family policy in Japan: Limited changes despite broad recognition of the declining fertility problem. *Journal of European Social Policy, 20*(5), 422–32.

Schultz, K. M. (2006). Secularization: A bibliographic essay. *The Hedgehog Review, 8*(1–2), 170–8.

Singh, G. K., & van Dyck, P. C. (2010). *Infant mortality in the U.S. 1935–2007*. HRSA. https://www.hrsa.gov/sites/default/files/healthitBACKUPJan6-17/HealthITArchive/images/mchb_infantmortality_pub.pdf

Smith, I., Sawkins, J. W., & Seaman, P. T. (1998). The economics of religious participation: A cross-country study. *Kyklos, 51*, 25–43.

Stark, R. (1999). Secularization, R.I.P. *Sociology of Religion, 60*(3), 249–73.

Stark, R., & Bainbridge, W. S. (1985). *The future of religion: Secularization, revival, and cult formation*. University of California Press.

Stark, R., & Bainbridge, W. S. (1987). *A theory of religion*. Lang.

Stark, R., & Finke, R. (2000). *Acts of faith: Explaining the human side of religion*. University of California Press.

Stark, R., & Iannaccone, L. (1994). A supply-side reinterpretation of the "secularization" of Europe. *Journal for the Scientific Study of Religion, 33*(3), 230–52.

Stimson, J. A. (1999). *Public Opinion in America: Moods Cycles and Swings* (2nd ed.). Boulder, CO: Westview Press.

Tawney, R. H. (1926). *Religion and the rise of capitalism: A historical study*.

te Grotenhuis, M., & Scheepers, P. (2001). Churches in Dutch: Causes of religious disaffiliation in the Netherlands, 1937–1995. *Journal for the Scientific Study of Religion, 40*, 591–606.

Teilhard de Chardin, P. (1959). *The phenomenon of man* (B. Wall, Trans.). Introduction by Julian Huxley. Harper and Brothers.

Thomas, S. M. (2005). *The global resurgence of religion and the transformation of international relations*. Palgrave Macmillan.

Thornhill, R., Fincher, C. L., & Aran, D. (2009). Parasites, democratization, and the liberalization of values across contemporary countries. *Biological Reviews, 84*(1), 113–31.

Thornhill, R., Fincher, C. L., Murray, D. R., & Schaller, M. (2010). Zoonotic and non-zoonotic diseases in relation to human personality and societal values. *Evolutionary Psychology, 8*, 151–5.

Tilly, C., & Wood, L. J. (2009). *Social movements, 1768–2008*. Paradigm.

Transparency International. (2019). *Corruption Perceptions Index*. https://www.transparency.org/files/content/pages/2019_CPI_Report_EN.pdf

Trevor-Roper, H. (1967). Religion, the Reformation and social change. In H. Trevor-Roper, *Religion, the Reformation and Social Change* (pp. 1–46).

TRT World. (2019, November 22). *Overwhelming majority of terror victims are Muslims*. https://www.trtworld.com/mea/overwhelming-majority-of-terror-victims-are-muslims-31586

United Nations. (2019). *Global study on homicide*. https://www.unodc.org/unodc/en/data-and-analysis/global-study-on-homicide.html#:~:text=As%20in%20previous%20years%2C%20the,the%20scale%20of%20homicide%20globally

United Nations Development Program. (2001–4). *Human development report, 2001–2004*. Oxford University Press.

United Nations Development Program. (2009). *Human development report 2007/2008*.

United Nations Development Program Human Development Reports. (2013). *The rise of the South*. United Nations.

United Nations Development Program Human Development Reports. (2019). *Beyond income, beyond averages, beyond today: Inequalities in human development in the 21st century*. United Nations. http://hdr.undp.org/en/2019-report

V-Dem Institute. (2019). *Democracy facing global challenges: V-Dem annual democracy report*. https://www.v-dem.net/media/filer_public/99/de/99dedd73-f8bc-484c-8b91-44ba601b6e6b/v-dem_democracy_report_2019.pdf

van Tubergen, F. (2013). Religious change of new immigrants in the Netherlands: The event of migration. *Social Science Research, 42*(3), 715–25.

van Tubergen, F, te Grotenhuis, M., & Ultee, W. (2005). Denomination, religious context, and suicide: Neo-Durkheimian multilevel explanations tested with individual and contextual data. *American Journal of Sociology, 111,* 797–823.

Verhoeven, W. J., Jansen, W., & Dessens, J. (2009). Losers in market transition: The unemployed, the retired, and the disabled. *European Sociological Review, 25*(1), 103–22.

Voas, D., & Chaves, M. (2016). Is the United States a counterexample to the secularization thesis? *American Journal of Sociology, 121*(5), 1517–56.

Voas, D., Olson, D. V. A., & Crockett, A. (2002). Religious pluralism and participation: Why previous research is wrong. *American Sociological Review, 67,* 212–30.

Voye, L., & Dobbelaere, K. (1994). Roman Catholicism: Universalism at stake. In R. Cipriani (Ed.), *Religions sans frontières?* (pp. 83–113). Dipartimento per L'Informazione e Editoria, Rome.

Wallace, A. F. C. (1966). *Religion: An anthropological view.* Random House.

Weber, M. (1930). *The Protestant ethic and the spirit of capitalism.* Scribner. (Original work published 1904–5)

Weber, M. (1993). *The sociology of religion.* Beacon. (Original work published 1922)

Wehner, P. (2019, July 5). The deepening crisis in evangelical Christianity: Support for Trump comes at a high cost for Christian witness. *The Atlantic.*

Weinberg, L., & Pedahzur, A. (2004). *Religious fundamentalism and political extremism.* Taylor and Francis.

Welzel, C. (2013). *Freedom rising: Human empowerment and the quest for emancipation.* Cambridge University Press.

Welzel, C., & Inglehart, R. F. (2016). Misconceptions of measurement equivalence: Time for a paradigm shift. *Comparative Political Studies, 49*(8), 1068–94.

Wendling, Z. A., Emerson, J. W., Esty, D. C., Levy, M. A., de Sherbinin, A., et al. (2018). *2018 Environmental Performance Index.* Yale Center for Environmental Law and Policy. https://sedac.ciesin.columbia.edu/data/set/epi-environmental-performance-index-2018

Wielander, G. (2013). *Christian Values in Communist China.* Routledge.

Wilson, D. S. (2002). *Darwin's cathedral: Evolution, religion, and the nature of society.* University of Chicago Press.

Wilson, D. S. (2005). Testing major evolutionary hypotheses about religion with a random sample. *Human Nature, 16*(4), 419–46.

Wilson, D. S., & Wilson, E. O. (2007, November 3). Evolution: Survival of the selfless. There's more to evolution than the selfish gene. *New Scientist,* pp. 42–6.

Woodberry, R. D. (1998). When surveys lie and people tell the truth. *American Sociological Review, 63,* 119–22.

World Bank. (2001). *World development indicators* [CD-ROM]. World Bank.

Wuthnow, R. (1998). *After heaven: Spirituality in America since the 1950s.* University of California Press.

Wuthnow, R. (2010). *After the baby boomers: How twenty- and thirty-somethings are shaping the future of American religion.* Princeton University Press.

Xu, C. (2011). The fundamental institutions of China's reforms and development. *Journal of Economic Literature, 49*(4), 1076–151.

Zhirkov, K., & Inglehart, R. (2019). Human security and religious change in 65 societies: An analysis of survey data across 1981–2014." HSE Sociology Working Paper Series. https://www.hse.ru/data/2019/12/16/1523559212/92SOC2019.pdf

Index

For the benefit of digital users, indexed terms that span two pages (e.g., 52–53) may, on occasion, appear on only one of those pages.

190 INDEX